John Corbin

The Elizabethan Hamlet

A Study of the Sources and of Shakspere's Environment...

John Corbin

The Elizabethan Hamlet
A Study of the Sources and of Shakspere's Environment...

ISBN/EAN: 9783743465022

Manufactured in Europe, USA, Canada, Australia, Japa

Cover: Foto ©Thomas Meinert / pixelio.de

Manufactured and distributed by brebook publishing software
(www.brebook.com)

John Corbin

The Elizabethan Hamlet

The Elizabethan Hamlet

THE ELIZABETHAN HAMLET

A Study of the Sources, and of Shakspere's Environment, to show that the Mad Scenes had a Comic Aspect now Ignored

By
JOHN CORBIN

With a Prefatory Note by
F. YORK POWELL
Regius Professor of Modern History, Oxford

FRVCTVS INTER FOLIA

Published in London by ELKIN MATHEWS
Vigo Street W.: and in New York by
CHARLES SCRIBNER'S SONS Fifth Avenue

M · D · CCC · XC · V

TO MY MOTHER

A Prefatory Note

Mr. John Corbin, of Harvard and Oxford, asks me to put a word or two at the front of his Essay. I have no special authority to speak on the subject, but I do not wish to decline his hospitality. When he showed me his work and we talked it over, it seemed to me that he had got hold of a truth that has not been clearly, if at all, expressed in our Elizabethan studies—to wit, that the 16th century audience's point of view, and, of necessity, the playwright's treatment of his subject, were very different from ours of to-day in many matters of mark. Just as the impossibility of getting women actors on the Globe stage must have cramped and hampered in some respects the dramatist's presentment of women, and tended to make him emphasize certain convenient types of feminine character, and omit or but briefly touch on others, thus affecting the drama as a complete presentment of life, so the attitude of an Elizabethan audience towards physical pain and mania has affected the plays of Shakspere and Webster and others in a way that is apt to puzzle the modern critic, especially if he be unfamiliar with the drama of other days and other lands. Hence, though I have had nothing to do with Mr. Corbin's conception of

vii

PREFATORY NOTE

or treatment of his subject, and have never given any
direction to his studies, I am so far responsible for the
present book that I advised him to print his Essay, as
his contribution to the study of a great subject; and this
responsibility I hereby acknowledge.

F. YORK POWELL

Oriel College, Oxford
Jan., 1895

The Elizabethan Hamlet

THE sense of Hamlet's reality has so impressed the critics that almost all of them
write as if he were an actual person, a recently deceased acquaintance; and assume
that, if they fail to reach a solution of the
problem his character presents, the fault
must of necessity lie in their analysis. But
Hamlet's reality is scarcely more remarkable
than the inconsistencies that, in spite of the
faith and zeal of the critics, have prevented
them from agreeing as to his character. One *The opposing*
man considers Hamlet great intellectually, *views of*
but malevolent; another takes him to be gentle *Hamlet*
and just, but lacking in courage; a third thinks
that, though he is not lacking in courage, his
intellect so overbalances his will that he re-
flects away the time for action; some hold
him quite sane, others make him wholly distraught : so that though all are impressed with
the reality of his character, hardly anyone is

satisfied with another's interpretation. Yet it is
to be noted that, contradictory as the interpretations are, they are to an amazing degree
based on the facts of the play. To one critic,
for instance, the marvellously vivid treatment of the Ghost is convincing evidence that
Hamlet is the great precursor of nineteenth
century spiritualistic faith. But, in spite of
not inconsis- his oath to remember his father's spirit,—
tent with the
text :
> Remember thee?
> Ay, thou poor ghost, while memory holds a seat
> In this distracted globe,—

he thinks of the hereafter only as

> The undiscover'd country, *from whose baurne*
> *No traveller returns.*

Another critic is obviously quite as well jus-
tified in finding Hamlet the precursor of
modern speculative doubt. One or two such
contradictions would not, of course, be hard
to reconcile ; but they are legion, and it is
notorious that no hypothesis, however well
founded on the facts of the play, has succeeded
in reconciling all of them.

To the historical student of Elizabethan
literature the question must arise whether

this disagreement does not spring in part at least from a want of knowledge of such mun- *A possible reason for this.* dane facts in Shakspere's life—the character of his audiences, and the conventional Elizabethan methods of play writing—as inevitably influence a dramatist's productions. We have Shakspere's own testimony, in the Sonnets, to the narrowness and hardship of his life and calling. He was a popular playwright in an age when the drama was as little reputable as our variety stage ; and similarly *Hamlet* was a popular tale told and re-told during four centuries, possessing scant literary and certainly no philosophical significance. Too little emphasis has been laid on this. The purpose of this essay is to study the play from the point of view of the gallants and 'prentices for whom Richard Burbage acted it,—to revivify the Elizabethan Hamlet.

The discussion will fall into five chief divisions. I shall consider first the Eliza- *The thesis outlined.* bethan sources of Shakspere's story. From these I shall hope to show not only that *Hamlet* was originally a crude tragedy of blood ; but also that certain phases of the story

—notably Hamlet's madness—were treated more comically in the versions preceding Shakspere's *Hamlet* than we can readily conceive. This will suggest my second consideration, a study of the comic sense of Elizabethan audiences, the actual public for which Shakspere wrote. This consideration will, I hope, confirm the first : it will show that to Shakspere's contemporaries many things—insanity, torture, and the like—now held repulsive or even tragic, were conventionally amusing ; and that consequently in the pre-Shaksperean play Hamlet's madness must have been an actual source of mirth. Thirdly, I shall consider certain peculiar features of Shakspere's environment and methods in writing which make it unlikely that he effaced wholly the traditional comic treatment of Hamlet's madness. This will lead to my fourth division, an exposition of certain of the most important scenes in old plays where madness is treated as a source of mirth, and of similar scenes in Shakspere. In my fifth and final division I shall present whatever evidence I shall have gathered

4

showing that there are distinct traces in the Hamlet familiar to modern readers of the comic treatment of madness, even in some of those scenes which from a modern point of view are most deeply tragic. Such a demonstration as I have outlined would account for the divergent views of the critics, and pave the way to a well grounded study of Shakspere's meaning.

I

PRE-SHAK-
SPEREAN
HAMLETS
The ultimate source of the plot of Hamlet is a tale in the *Historiæ Danicæ* of Saxo Grammaticus, who wrote as early as the twelfth century. Other early versions are found, but the earliest known to Shakspere was probably the prose *Hystorie of Hamblet*, which was written, in French, by Belleforest, in 1570. On the basis of this *Hystorie* an English play was written not later than 1589. This play is now lost ; but we have two plays which were founded directly upon it. The first of these is a German version, *Fratricide Punished*, and the second is Shakspere's earliest extant version, the first quarto *Hamlet*. This was printed piratically in 1603. In the following year the second quarto was printed authentically. This is to all intents and purposes the modern *Hamlet*.

The *Hystorie of Hamblet* was thus written thirty-odd years before Shakspere's first quarto ; and there is little doubt that it

6

was translated into English almost immediately, so great was its popularity. The
earliest extant edition, moreover, is dated
1608, four years later than Shakspere's second
quarto. Its popularity, accordingly, was not
only immediate but, in spite of the success of
the play on the same subject, was sustained.
This fact will be of the utmost importance in
judging of the influence it exerted on the
dramatic versions of the story. No better
brief summary of it can be given than that
contained in the headings of the chapters,
and in the marginal notes. These I have
combined, inserting here and there a word to
explain the narrative by connecting it with
Shakspere's *Hamlet;* but I have kept as far
as possible to the literal wording of the
original.

'CHAP. I. How Horvendile [King Hamlet] *1. The 'Hys-*
and Fengon [Claudius] were made Governours *torie of Hamblet'*
of the Province of Ditmarse, and how Hor-
vendile marryed Geruth, [Queen Gertrude]
the daughter to [the] chief K. of Denmark,
by whom he had Hamblet : and how after
his marriage his brother Fengon slewe him

trayterously, and incestuously marryed his brothers wife, and what followed.

'CHAP. II. How Hamblet counterfeited the mad man, making many subtill answeres to escape the tyrannie of his uncle, and how he was tempted by a woman (through his uncles procurement) who thereby thought to undermine the Prince, and by that meanes to finde out whether he counterfeited madnesse or not: and how Hamblet would by no meanes bee brought to consent unto her, and what followed.

'CHAP. III. How Fengon [Claudius], uncle to Hamblet, a second time to intrap him in his politick madnes, caused one of his counsellors [Polonius] to be secretly hidden in the queenes chamber, behind the arras, to heare what speeches passed between Hamblet and the Queen; and how Hamblet killed him, and escaped that danger, and what followed.

'CHAP. IIII. How Fengon [Claudius] the third time devised to send Hamblet to the king of England, with secret letters to have him put to death: and how Hamblet, when his companions [Rosencrantz and Guildenstern] slept, read the letters, and instead of them counterfeited others, willing the king of England to put the two messengers to death, and to marry his daughter to Hamblet, which was effected; and how Hamblet escaped out of England.

'CHAP. V. How Hamblet, having escaped out of England, arrived in Denmarke the same day that the Danes were celebrating his funerals, supposing him to be dead in England; and how he revenged his fathers death upon his uncle and the rest of the courtiers; and what followed.'

Some idea of the inexpressible brutality *a tale of murder and* of this story may be had in the few citations *revenge,* for which I have space. The importance of these passages will lie in the fact that the *Hystorie* afforded the ground-plan upon which the lost play was constructed. The feigned madness of Hamblet is thus described:

' Every day beeing in the queenes palace, . . . hee rent and tore his clothes, wallowing and lying in the durt and mire, his face all filthy and blacke, running through the streets like a man distraught, not speaking one worde, but such as seemed to proceede of madnesse and meere frenzie ; all his actions and jestures beeing no other than the right countenances of a man wholly deprived of all reason and understanding, in such sort, that as then hee seemed fitte for nothing but to make sport to the pages and ruffling courtiers that attended in the court of his uncle and father-in-law.' Hamblet's revenge is accomplished as follows : Hamblet 'seeing those drunken bodies, filled with wine, lying like hogs upon the ground, some sleeping, others vomiting the over great abundance of wine which without measure they had swallowed up, made the hangings about the hall to fall downe and cover them all over ; which he nailed to the ground . . . in such sort, that . . . it was unpossible to get from under them : and presently he set fire in the foure corners of the hal, in such sort, that all that were as then therein not one escaped away, but were forced to purge their sins by fire, and dry up the great abundance of liquor by them received into their bodies.'

This revenge he completed by giving the King 'such a blowe upon the chine of the necke, that hee cut his head cleane from his shoulders.'

The probable influence of such passages upon the play may best be explained by reference to one of the most striking conventions of Elizabethan tragedy, the comic underplot. The necessity of blending the humorous with the pathetic—so thoroughly acknowledged by modern writers — was dimly recognized by the earlier English dramatists. Their first crude device was to introduce among the tragic events a series of comic scenes. These were usually quite distinct from the main action. Many of the most celebrated old dramas may be divided into two plays, a pure comedy and an unmixed tragedy, each complete in itself. Certain of the dramatists, however, and prominent among them Shakspere, seem to have felt the awkwardness of this device ; for, instead of the consistent underplot, they introduced stray comic scenes having a direct connection with the main plot, of which the Porter's scene in *Macbeth* and the Grave Diggers' in *Hamlet* are notable instances. They led, no doubt, to the more artistic method of mingling comedy and tragedy in the same scene—of which the serio-comic relationship between Lear and his Fool is an excellent example. But this was a later development,— at the time when the lost play was written it was unknown.

in which Hamlet's brutal madness

As the *Hystorie* contained no series of scenes upon which to construct a comic underplot, we must look to its few amusing incidents for a hint as to the basis of the comedy in the lost play. The foul humour of Hamblet's mock madness is frankly alleged by the author to have made 'sport to pages and ruffling courtiers;' and in the account of Hamblet's revenge upon the courtiers and upon the King there is a brutal humour, a savage sarcasm, which any one familiar with rudimentary human nature will recognize, revolting as it is to our conventional humanity. The intelligent playwright could scarcely have failed to take the hint to derive his comedy from these scenes. But herein lies

12

the significant point: If he did so, those *supplies the place of comic underplot.* incidents which in the second quarto, the familiar *Hamlet*, are most tragic, must, in the lost play, have had a distinct comic aspect.

This paradox is even more clearly suggested in another scene. A certain lady in the *Hystorie* is set to tempt Hamblet carnally 'through his uncles procurement,' in a solitary wood. It is thus to be discovered, to the lady and to courtiers in ambush, whether he is really mad. This is the germ of the Hamlet-Ophelia scene in Shakspere, which has probably been more variously interpreted and less understood than any other tragic scene in literature. The lady was a 'faire and beawtifull woman' to whom the Prince was 'wholy . . . in affection.' As she too had 'from her infancy loved and favoured him, . . . [she] informed [him] of the treason' intended against him. Nevertheless, she was 'exceeding sorrowfull . . . to leave his companie without injoying the pleasure of his body, whome shee loved more than herselfe,' and essayed, though in vain, to tempt Hamblet.

13

The upshot of all this was that 'the prince in this sort having both deceived the courtiers, and the ladyes expectation, that affirmed and swore that hee never once offered to have his pleasure of the woman, although in subtilty hee affirmed the contrary, every man there upon assured themselves that without *The origin of* all doubt he was distraught of his sences.' *the Hamlet-* The situation is in a measure obscured by *Ophelia scene.* the lack of the context, and by the involution of the sentences ; but it is briefly this : When the lady was eager, Hamblet rebuffed her ; but when she admitted to the King that Hamblet had not satisfied her 'expectation,' he insisted falsely that he had. Either of these actions was, to the courtiers and the King, proof positive of his insanity. His purpose in all this was the very serious one of escaping the peril in which he lay ; but in executing it he turned the tables so neatly on both the 'beawtifull lady' and the King that the situation remains to this day vulgarly amusing. Yet in the second quarto this scene is, under our modern interpretation, one of the most deeply tragic in literature.

14

Though this *Hystorie* is quite alien in spirit to the second quarto, it contains most, though not all, of the incidents there. It probably contains too the suggestions of others. The incident of Hamblet's mock burial may have suggested the true burial of Ophelia; and his successful oration to the people may have suggested the idea of making Laertes appear at the head of a popular insurrection. The incidents the *Hystorie* lacks are the play within the play, the grave-digging scene, and chiefly the idea of making the murder of Hamblet's father secret, thus introducing the Ghost. *Shakspere's debt to the 'Hystorie.'*

So much for the *Hystorie*. We have now to ascertain as far as possible the nature of the lost play founded upon it. *2. The lost play* In the first place, the brutality of the *Hystorie* makes it not unlikely that the lost play was a tragedy of blood—after the kind of Kyd's *Spanish Tragedy*, or Shakspere's *Titus Andronicus*. In the second place, the fact that Hamblet's subtly pretended madness was used throughout the *Hystorie* to amuse the reader, even in those scenes

15

which in the first and second quartos appear to us most deeply tragic, suggests that they may have been utilised in the lost play to supply the lack of comic underplot. It will at least be interesting to keep an eye open for evidence upon these two points.

antedating the first quarto by fourteen years,

The date of the lost play is fixed by contemporary allusions as not later than 1589, fourteen years before the publication of Shakspere's earliest known version. These allusions give some clue to its character. Nash, in an epistle prefaced to Greene's *Menaphon*, printed in 1589, says, 'English *Seneca* read by Candle-light, yeelds many good sentences, as *Bloud is a begger*, and so forth : and if you intreate him faire in a frosty morning, hee will affoord you whole Hamlets, I should say handfuls of Tragicall speeches.' In *Wits Miserie*, 1596, Thomas Lodge, speaking of an 'incarnate diuel,' says that he 'looks as pale as the Visard of ye ghost which cried so miserally at ye Theator like an oister wife, *Hamlet, reuenge.*' In Dekker's *Satiro-mastix*, printed in 1602, the year previous to the publication of the first

16

quarto, we find :—'*Asini*. Wod I were hang'd if I can call you any names but Captaine and Tucca. *Tuc.* No Fye'st, my name's Hamlet reuenge : thou hast been at Parris garden hast not?' This phrase, 'Hamlet, revenge!' which Shakspere saw fit to omit in his version, had made so deep an impression on the popular mind that years passed before the extant treatment of the scene effaced it. In Dekker's *Westward Hoe*, published in 1607, four years after the publication of Shakspere's first quarto, we find :—'I but when light Wiues make heauy husbands, let these husbands play mad *Hamlet ;* and crie reuenge.' So likewise in Rowland's *The Night Raven*, 1618, fifteen years after the first quarto :

I will not cry *Hamlet Reuenge* my greeues,
But I will call *Hang-man Reuenge* on theeues.

What first strikes one in these allusions is that in the lost play the Ghost's demand *ridiculed for* for revenge impressed the public as blatant ; *its rant,* and blatancy is very foreign to the moral dignity of Shakspere's Ghost. The allusions contain, moreover, a vein of contempt and

17   D

satire. In this they resemble nothing so much as the allusions to certain extant tragedies of blood, the popularity of which was quite equal to that of the early *Hamlet.* For instance, in the Introduction to *Bartholomew Fair,* Ben Jonson says: 'Hee that will sweare, *Ieronimo,* or *Andronicus,* are the best playes, yet, shall passe vnexcepted at, heere, as a man whose iudgment shewes it is constant, and hath stood still, these fiue and twentie, or thirtie yeeres. Though it be an *Ignorance,* it is a vertuous and stay'd ignorance ; and next to *truth,* a confirm'd errour does well ; such a one the *Author* knowes where to finde him.' The satire of this is obvious. Both in the phrases from the lost play, and in *and apparently* the manner in which they are quoted, we *a tragedy of* have very strong confirmation that the play *blood.* was a tragedy of blood.

The next step in fixing the character of the lost play is to study the two extant versions founded directly upon it, the German version and the first quarto of Shakspere. From the point of view of these versions we shall discover further evidence that the

18

lost play was a tragedy of blood, and moreover, that in it the comic passages I have
pointed out in the *Hystorie* were used to
supply the place of an underplot.

The German version contains the bloody *3. The Ger-*
incidents of the *Hystorie* so augmented as to *man Hamlet*
present the main points of the first quarto :
the secret fratricide, the incestuous marriage,
the Ghost, Hamlet's feigned madness, the
play within the play, the voyage to England,
Ophelia's distraction and death, Laertes' re-
turn, the foul fencing bout, and the poisoned
drink. The only important scenes omitted are
those between Hamlet and the two courtiers,
Rosencrantz and Guildenstern, the Grave-
diggers' scene, and the scene at Ophelia's
grave.

In spite, however, of this close agree-
ment in plot, the play appears, at first reading,
debased beyond all kinship to Elizabethan
literature—so barren of interest, so unutter-
ably coarse in every detail, as to be a
thorn in the side of the lover of Shakspere's
Hamlet.

A fair idea of its puerility may be had

in the scene which corresponds to the episode, found in all English versions, of the voyage to England and the killing of the King's emissaries. This episode is presented in the German play with a childish striving after stage effect. Hamlet is represented on an island, about to be killed at the King's order by bandits. At the last moment he says :

'Ham. Hear me—one word more. . . I . . beg you to let me raise to my Maker a fervent prayer ; after that I am ready to die. But I will give you a signal : I will turn my hands toward heaven, and the moment I stretch out my arms, fire! Aim both pistols at my sides, and when I say "Shoot!" give me as much as I need, and be sure to hit me so that I shall not be long in torture.' . . . Then '(*spreading out his hands*) Shoot! (*throwing himself forward on his face between the two, who shoot each other*). Oh just Heaven! thanks be to thee for this angelic idea! . . . But these villains,—as was their work, so is their pay. The dogs are still stirring ; they have shot each other. But out of revenge I will give them a death-

hopelessly per- verted in seem- ing,

blow to make sure . . . (*Stabs them with their own swords*).' *Act IV., Scene I.*

The treatment of the Ghost offers a similar instance. The First Sentinel, as he leaves the platform, admits that he has been frightened by a ghost, and is glad enough to go home. The second sentinel makes fun of him, but is presently himself overtaken. The Majesty of buried Denmark '*from behind gives him a box on the ear, and makes him drop his musket, and exit.*' 'The devil himself is after me,' he exclaims. 'Oh, I am so frightened, I can't stir!' *Act I., Scene II.*

e.g. Hamlet's escape, and the Ghost scene,

In both of these scenes, and to a like degree throughout the play, the tragic incidents of Shakspere's *Hamlet* are told with an eye to comic effect, and we have the anomaly of a tragedy of blood, crude and revolting, in which the majority of the scenes are given an element of horseplay, or sport.

There is in this fact at least a suggestion of kinship to the *Hystorie of Hamblet.* And a close study of the text will show that the remoteness of the German version from Shakspere's versions is chiefly in seem-

ing. To begin with, this very scene contains the Ghost's famous speeches from the
'cellarage,'—'Sweare. Sweare.'—those 'sub-
terraneous speeches' which, in Shakspere,
Coleridge found 'hardly defensible'; and the
comic treatment of the Ghost is recalled in
Shakspere's 'Well said, old Mole, can'st worke
in the earth? so fast.' This phrase, and other
similar ones in the same scene, Moberly calls
'a strange and baffling jest,' and Coleridge 'a
wild transition to the ludicrous.' The German
version taken as a whole, moreover, contains
sufficient points in common with Shakspere's
versions to convince the critics that it is
more nearly related to the first than to the
second quarto, and to the lost version than
to either. As most of the evidence of this
is textual, we need not linger over it. There
are one or two points of resemblance, however, that will later be extremely significant
of the peculiar character of the lost play, and
of the extent to which it was related to the
first quarto.

In the German version, in the scene
between Hamlet and Ophelia where the King

and his Counsellor are secretly listening, Hamlet feigns madness as in the first quarto, but the treatment of the scene is as follows :

'*Oph.* I pray your highness to take back the jewel which you presented to me.

'*Ham.* What, girl! wouldst thou have a husband? Get thee away from me ; nay, come here. Hearken, girl, you young women do nothing but lead young fellows astray. Your beauty you buy of the apothecaries and peddlers. Listen, I will tell you a story. There was a cavalier in Anion who fell in love with a lady, who, to look at, was the goddess Venus. However, when bedtime came, the bride went first and began to undress herself. First, she took out an eye which had been set in very cunningly ; then her front teeth, made of ivory, so cleverly that the like were not to be seen ; then she washed herself, and off went all the paint with which she had smeared herself. At last, when the bridegroom came and thought to embrace her, the moment he saw her he started back, and thought it was a spectre. And thus it is that you deceive the young

23

fellows; therefore listen to me. But stay, girl! No, go to a nunnery, but not to a *yet having stri-* nunnery where two pairs of slippers lie at *king points in* the bedside. [*Exit.*
common with
the lost play; '*Cor.* (*Polonius*). Is he not perfectly and veritably mad, gracious lord and King?

'*King.* Corambus, leave us. . . [*Exit Corambus.*] . . It seems to us that this is not genuine madness, but rather a feigned madness.' *Act II., Scene IV.*

This is hardly a literal rendering of the episode in the *Hystorie;* but in spirit it is precisely similar. In both versions Hamlet, in order to escape the espionage of the King, hoaxes Ophelia under the guise of madness; and in both the humour is, according to modern standards, indecent. The difference between the two, moreover, is merely that which must necessarily have existed between the narrative and the dramatic version of such an episode, for even in pre-Shaksperean England the passage in the *Hystorie* could not have been represented literally on the Stage. The scene is, to be sure, totally different in spirit from our conception of the parallel

24

scene in the first quarto. Yet it has points of similarity that in the scientific study of literature pass for more than such arguments as appeal merely to the æsthetic or moral senses. It has certain striking words and phrases that recur almost literally in Shakspere. 'Your beauty you buy of the apothecaries and peddlers,' is the Shaksperean Hamlet's 'I haue heard of your paintings too, God has giuen you one face, And you make your selues another.' 'To a Nunnery goe,' is identical; and there are other expressions, to be discussed later, which read like paraphrases of Shakspere.

All this has an important bearing upon the lost play: It is beyond the remotest possibility that so many speeches should by mere chance be identical in both the versions to which it gave rise, the German and the Shak- *and being in reality closely* sperean *Hamlets.* The proof is positive that *akin to it:* in letter and in spirit the lost play had vastly more in common with the German version than at first appears.

The three versions thus far discussed, the *Hystorie*, the lost play, and the German

The points of similarity. play, form, it is now evident, a closely connected series. I have shown that in the first and third members of the series certain scenes were amusing which in the first quarto and second quarto appear quite serious. The hypothesis that in the intermediate version, the lost play, these scenes were amusing is, to say the least, worthy of further discussion.

The evidence of Shakspere's first quarto upon the lost play, and upon the comic element I have supposed in it, is now in order. The character of the first quarto as a whole may best be shown by stating first in what respects it resembles Shakspere's final version, and then in what it differs from this. The *4. Shakspere's* two quartos are alike in seriousness and ele- *first version :* vation of style. The story how Hamlet outwitted the factors of the King is told with fitting sobriety and probability. The Ghost is essentially a poetic creation, and full of ghostly dignity. Hamlet's pretended madness strikes us as shrewd and trenchant ; but apparently those scenes in which it gives rise to comic or amusing situations have to do only

26

with Polonius, Rosencrantz, and Guildenstern
—characters feebly developed in the German
play—and with Osric, upon whom Hamlet
repeats in a bettered form the mad jests which
in the German version he played off on a certain Phantasmo. When Hamlet speaks to *Its resemblance*
Ophelia, it is apparently with predominant *to the final ver-*
seriousness and tragic effect. In only one *sion ;*
passage is there the least suggestion of
comedy.

'*Ham.*   Where's thy father?
'*Ofel.*   At home my lord.
'*Ham.*   For Gods sake let the doores be
          shut on him,
He may play the foole no where but in his
Owne house: to a Nunnery goe.' *Line 873.*
The fact that Polonius is 'close in the study,'
straining to catch what Hamlet says, gives this
speech an inevitably comic aspect. Still under
no circumstances could the scene as a whole in
the first quarto strike us, from a modern point
of view, as anything but essentially tragic.

Having conjectured that in the old play
this and other similar scenes bore a largely
comic character, we are forced, at least for the

present, to assume that Shakspere sacrificed this almost completely. This supposition, it must be admitted, is confirmed by the fact that in Hamlet's scenes of feigned madness with Rosencrantz and Guildenstern—not found in the German versions—and with Polonius— barely suggested there—we find enough of wit and of comedy of character to compensate for the predominant seriousness of the once comic scenes.

its points of difference ; Passing to the differences between Shakspere's two quartos, we find that in the first quarto, though the incidents and scenes are the same, the phrasing is far less finished and beautiful. The character of Hamlet, moreover, is fully conceived only where he is in action. The contemplative side is barely suggested. In fine, the first quarto, though a very good acting play, lacks all that makes *Hamlet Hamlet.* By no possibility can we take the Prince to be more than a dignified stage rendering of the crude Hamblet of the *Hystorie.* The first quarto, as several of the critics have said, is to be regarded not so much as an early bit of Shakspere's workmanship as the

28

work of a very inferior artist. Clarke and Wright conclude that it is 'an older play,' composed of a distinctly tragic treatment of the incidents of both the German version and the *Hystorie;* but that it is still 'in a tran- *its close rela-* sition state ; . . . it was undergoing a re- *tionship to the* modelling, but had not received more than *lost play.* the first rough touches of the great master's hand.' If we knew no other Shaksperean version than the first quarto, there would be little or nothing paradoxical in supposing that the most serious episodes in which Hamlet moves had, in the lost play upon which it was founded, been wilfully buffooned.

We have now at hand the chief facts that bear upon the lost play. The main features of its source, the *Hystorie*, we found, were a series of incidents such as a dramatist would be likely to choose for a tragedy of blood ; and the allusions to the lost play strengthen the supposition. There was no suggestion of a comic underplot ; but there was interwoven with the tragic incidents a series of partly amusing situations brought about by the fact that the hero, though sane,

29

was expected to act the madman ; and these were of a character to supply the place of comic underplot in the lost play. In the German *Hamlet*, which was based upon the lost play, we found that the bloodily tragic incidents,—contained also, presumably, in the lost play,—were debased and considerably augmented. Moreover, the comic treatment of all phases of Hamlet's pretended madness, which, judging from the character of the *Hystorie*, might have afforded the comic relief to the lost play, was likewise reproduced. Upon this fact we founded the hypothesis that they were similarly treated in the lost play. When we came to Shakspere's first quarto— the lost play remodelled—we found the same bloodily tragic incidents ; but they were treated with greater sobriety and artistic reserve ; while several of the scenes which, in the *Hystorie* and the German version, had been used to enliven the gloom, no longer appeared comic. Still even in these scenes there were distinct traces of the old comic treatment.

From the data thus summarised no conclusion is admissible that would not make the lost play a tragedy of blood. Nor does it take the ghost of the lost play to tell us this. *The evidence as to the lost play summarized.* A number of the critics have observed that *Hamlet* presents an aspect which throws it back into the school of *The Spanish Tragedy;* and the most recent work on this subject, Gregor Sarrazin's *Thomas Kyd and his Circle,* which has come to me since writing the foregoing, proves beyond reasonable doubt that the lost play was by Kyd; was conceived as a companion piece to *Jeronimo* and *The Spanish Tragedy;* and contained, in a slightly altered form, the events and situations of both of these plays. Likewise no conclusion is admissible that would make the prince Hamlet of the lost play anything but a person who feigned madness to escape the jealousy of a usurping uncle; and our evidence would forbid our regarding this feigned madness as of such a nature it could not be turned to comic effect in the less tragic scenes. Even on this point we might say to the ghost of the lost play : ' Rest, rest, perturbed spirit ! ' for we have the combined

testimony of Dr. Maginn and Dr. Johnson that
this is the case even with Shakspere's final
version. ' I doubt if . . . the English
vulgar . . . could abide [Hamlet] without . . . having Polonius buffooned for
him, and, to no small extent, Hamlet himself ;
as he always was whenever I saw the part
played, and as the *great critic*, Dr Johnson,
would seem to think he ought to be. For
he says, "the pretended madness of Hamlet
causes much mirth ! ! !" '

The really significant facts in the evidence gathered thus far relate to the comic
aspect of Hamlet's madness in those scenes
which in our familiar version appear purely
tragic. In the *Hystorie*, Hamblet's most
bestial pretence of madness amused 'pages
Hamlet's mad- and ruffling courtiers,' and in the episode
ness everywhere with the ' beawtifull lady' he used his sham
comic. madness as a stalking-horse for a most
outrageous bit of hoaxing. In the German
version, the scene founded upon this episode
with the ' beawtifull lady ' bears a precisely
similar spirit of vulgar mirth ; and the action
of the scene differs only as it would neces-

32

sarily differ in a dramatic handling. In the first quarto, although the spirit is apparently quite different, there is in this scene and elsewhere a close verbal relationship with the German version ; and there is also some slight trace of comedy. All this suggests my main hypothesis, and at the same time powerfully substantiates it, namely, that in the lost play Hamlet's feigned madness bore a comic aspect in certain of those scenes which, as they appear in the modern Hamlet, strike us as most deeply tragic.

This hypothesis presumes in Elizabethan audiences an attitude toward acts of cruelty and insanity which is incredible to any one brought up amid the sensibility of modern life. Yet there is much evidence that it is thoroughly in accord with the characteristics of Elizabethan England and of the Elizabethan Drama. Until this state of things is made clear, the discussion of the comic element in Shakspere's first quarto must wait.

II

It is a fact too often forgotten that bear baiting was a national sport with our forefathers, and that the merriment of their dinner tables was supplied by idiots and madmen. Hentzner, a German who visited England in 1598, describes the manner of bear baiting.

'There is still another place,' he records, 'built in the form of a Theatre, which serves for the baiting of Bulls and Bears, they are fastned behind, and then worried by great English bull-dogs; but not without great risque to the dogs, from the horns of the one, and the teeth of the other; and it sometimes happens they are killed upon the spot; fresh ones are immediately supplied in the places of those that are wounded, or tired. To this entertain-
ment, there often follows that of whipping a blinded bear, which is performed by five or six men, standing circularly with whips, which they exercise upon him without any mercy, as he cannot escape from them because of his chain;

he defends himself with all his force and skill, throwing down all who come within his reach, and are not active enough to get out of it, and tearing the whips out of their hands, and breaking them.'

Such were the pastimes of our ancestors; but whether the brutality of the spectacle *Bear baiting.* made serious sport, like the unexampled physical strain of an University boat-race, or whether it provoked laughter, is not stated. In the bear-baiting it seems natural to assume that the element of serious sport predominated. As for the spectacle of five or six men scuffling and tussling with a blinded bear, this supposition scarcely holds. Spectators to whom the combats of dogs and tied bears was serious sport could hardly have been above hearty laughter when an unwary fellow was sent sprawling by a cuff on the side of the head.

About the humorous delight in madmen there is no possibility of doubt. A passage already quoted from the *Hystorie* shows that Hamblet's madness was considered fit sport for 'pages and ruffling courtiers;' and in a

35

The Court Fool quaint volume called '*A Nest of Ninnies,*
a bonâ fide *Simply of themselues without Compound,*' we
idiot. have superabundant evidence that partial and
even total insanity amused the Elizabethans.
The book is by one Robert Armin,—a pro-
fessional, who was certainly a member of
Shakspere's company, and probably at times
took the part of Dogberry. A thorough
understanding of the position which the idiots
Armin describes occupied in the Elizabethan
household can be attained—if at all—only by
reading the entire volume ; but the following
siftings must serve.

'A kinde gentleman . . . had a foole,
Leonard they call him. . . . The Gentleman . . . hauing bought a goodly fayre
Hawke, brought her home, being not a little
proud of his penny-worth, and at Supper to
other Gentlemen, fell a praysing of her. . . .
Leonard standing by with his finger in his
mouth, as it was his custome, often hearing
them praise the goodnesse of the Hawke,
thought indeede they had meant for goodnesse
being farre better meate then a Turkey or a
Swan, was very desirous to eate of the same :

and vnknowne goes downe, and sodainely from
the pearch snatch the Hawke, and hauing
wrung off her neck, begins to besiedge that good
morsell, but with so good a courage, that the
feathers had almost choakt him : but there lay
my friend *Leonard* in a lamentable taking.
Well, the Hawke was mist, and the deede was
found, the Maister was fecht, and al men
might see the Hawk, feathers and all not
very wel disgested : there was no boote to bid
runne for drams to driue downe this vndisgested
moddicome : the Gentleman of the one side,
cryed hang the Foole, the Foole on the other
side cryed not, but made signes that his Hawke
was not so good as hee did praise her for : and
though the Gentleman loued his Hawke, yet he
loued the Foole aboue : being enforced rather
to laugh at his simplicitie, then to vere at his
losses sodainely : Being glad to make himselfe
merry, jested on it ever after.'

A more pitiable fool was Jack Miller, whom
Armin says he knew personally. This Miller
stuttered frightfully, and one of his most ludicrous performances was to sing songs full of difficult consonants. Once when he was amusing a

table of 'Gallants and Gentlewomen, almost the
state of the Country,' there was a lady present
who seems to have had our modern sense of
the impropriety of laughing.   That she was
very far in advance of her century, however,
is evident in Armin's narrative of the way her
sense of propriety was brought into ridicule.

'The Gallants and Gentlewomen . . .
especially . . . entreated him for his new
speach of the Pees : which he began in such
manner to speake, with driueling and stutter-
ing, that they began mightely to laugh : inso-
much that one proper Gentlewoman among the
rest, because shee would not seeme too immodest with laughing : for such is the humour of
many, that thinke to make all, when God knowes
they marre all : so shee, straining her selfe,
though inwardly she laughed hartely, gaue
out such an earnest of her modesty, that all
the Table rung of it.   Who is that, sayes one?
Not I, sayes another : but by her cheeks you
might find guilty *Gilbert*, where he had hid
the brush.   .   .   .   Thus simple *Jack* made
mirth to all, made the wisest laugh, but to
this day gathered little wit to himselfe.'

A lady in advance of her Century.

38

In the facts here brought forward there is nothing new ; but any one who has read far in criticism of the Elizabethan drama will testify that an analysis has not yet been made of the archaic taste in comedy which such primitive humor implied. I have already shown by the internal evidence of the three early versions of the story that in the lost play the (to us) cruel acts of madness, in such scenes as the Hamlet-Ophelia scene for instance, were probably meant by the playwright to be amusing. It is obvious in the evidence just presented that such a treatment would have been precisely in accordance with the tastes of the Elizabethans. Henceforth I shall take it for proved that, in the lost play, the Hamlet-Ophelia scene was treated with at least one eye to comic effect. Those who are still unconvinced I shall leave to consider parallel scenes, to be presented by and by, which were written by Shakspere's contemporaries, and even by Shakspere himself. For the present I shall attempt to estimate the influence of the lost play in general, and of the scenes of archaic comedy in particular, upon the first quarto.

Hamlet's madness comic in the lost play.

39

III

The influence of the lost play would, of course, have been very slight indeed if Shakspere were in the habit of remodelling carefully and thoroughly the plots upon which he worked. If, however, he were accustomed to work hastily, merely rephrasing scenes which he found already made to his hand, the influence would have been far from slight. The evidence on this point is fortunately well authenticated and digested. That Shakspere took his plots from older plays and novels, and often took them *in toto*, is a commonplace of the primers. All but two of the thirty-seven extant plays are known to have been thus constructed. The hasty and hap-hazard way in which Elizabethan playwrights worked is also well known. Henslowe's famous diary attests that the audiences of the time required a new play about every eighteen days on an average, including Sundays, and that the rapidity with which plays were written is most remarkable

THE ELIZABETHAN HAMLET

This is shown beyond dispute by the portions *The rewriting* of the diary where, among other charges, *of plays hasty and hap-* Henslowe registers the sums paid to play- *hazard.* wrights, the dates of the payment, and the authors who received the money. Nothing was more common than for two and even three or four dramatists to work together on one play. All this is as far as possible from the manner of writing such modern plays or novels as are in the least comparable with the best work of the Elizabethans.

It is also fairly well established that Shakspere often retouched and developed his work after the first 'run.' Different quartos of several of the plays show various readings which indicate this ; and of two plays at least, *Romeo and Juliet*, and *Hamlet*, we have two widely different Shaksperean versions. This evidence is particularly significant in view of the fact that no play was ever willingly given out in print until it had died a natural death on the boards. That we have even these two first drafts is due to accident, for they were pirated, as were several of the quartos that give various readings. If the pirates had been willing and able to print the first version of all the dramas, we should probably find that it was *The reason for the influence of Shakspere's sources.* Shakspere's custom in working over old plays, first to make a thorough revision, and then to rewrite and improve this if its success on the boards warranted. Under such conditions as these, only quite new plays could be written, as with us, in accordance with a consciously precise structure, a settled conception of character, an idea or purpose which moulds the events : the mass of the playwright's work sprang, with only such coherence and form as he might import into it, from the plot or scenes that formed his material.

Such a method in writing would be sufficient in itself to show that the influence of the lost play upon the first quarto must have been very strong ; but there is still greater reason why the dramatist should have followed the earlier play, in the known prestige of the story. The prose Hamlet had probably been familiar to Shakspere's audience for upward of thirty years ; and a new edition was put out five years after Shakspere's play was printed. The lost play likewise is known to

have been popular for at least thirteen years ;
to what extent is shown in the fact that its
peculiar phrases crop out in contemporary *The prestige of the pre-Shaksperean Hamlets.*
allusions years after they were altered in
Shakspere's first quarto. Let the reader ask
himself now how he feels when a new interpretation of any well known personage in
literature is presented. Does he relish the
adventurer Columbus, the moralist Macchia-
velli, or the immoral Washington ? No other
writer, moreover, is so thoroughly at the mercy
of the traditions and caprices of his contemporaries as the dramatist. And Shakspere
was no exception. Play upon play might be
cited, showing that for reasons of haste or
policy, or both, he left whole episodes that
savor of the cruder aspects of the Elizabethan
drama unrefined.

The crudities in Hamlet are not far to
seek. It is a significant fact that more than
one of the most clear-sighted of the critics
have found the Prince anything but the
'sweet' or 'gentle' youth of the effusive
commentators. Dr. Johnson says : Hamlet
'plays the madman most when he treats

43

Ophelia with so much rudeness, which seems to be useless and wanton cruelty.' And Steevens adds, ' He defers his purpose [of revenge] till he can find an opportunity of taking his uncle when he is least prepared for death, that he may insure damnation to his soul. Though he assassinated Polonius by accident, yet he deliberately procures the execution of his school-fellows, Rosencrantz and Guildenstern. . . . . Their end (as he declares in subsequent conversation with Horatio) gives him no concern, for they obtruded themselves into the service, and he thought he had a right to destroy them. From his brutal conduct toward Ophelia he is not less accountable for her distraction and death. He interrupts the funeral designed in honor of this lady. . . . He insults the brother of the dead, and boasts of an affection for his sister, which, before, he had denied to her face.' That either Dr. Johnson or Steevens presents a sympathetic view of Hamlet's character few will be hardy enough to insist; but any candid reader will admit that every one of their charges, like either of

The crudities in Hamlet

44

the opposing theories with regard to Shakspere's spiritual ideas, is substantiated by the
facts of the story ; and that these facts have
never been satisfactorily reconciled.

If, now, we consider the manifold con- *an inheri-*
sequences of the growth of the play through *tance from the*
the successive versions, a few, at least, of the *blood.*
inconsistencies will be accounted for. Take,
for instance, the Ghost episode. This, it will
be remembered, does not occur in the *Hystorie.* Its introduction into the lost play is
doubtless due to Thomas Kyd, and sprang,
in all probability, like that of Andrea's Ghost
into Kyd's *Spanish Tragedy*, from the desire
to make a telling scene, and incidentally to
emphasize the hero's duty of revenge. How
striking the scene proved in the lost play
is witnessed by the constant recurrence of
the Ghost's phrase, 'Hamlet, Revenge!' in
the books of the times. When, now, the
prince was made the instrument of a re- *The develop-*
vengeful spirit, it is evident that he had to *ment of the*
Ghost episode.
be represented as a creature of far greater
dignity than the Hamblet of the *Hystorie.* In
an acting drama, too, the guise of clownish

45

imbecility, which was made so much of in the prose narrative, would, in the long run, be monotonous. His demonstrations of insanity had to be made chiefly mental. Thus, for a double reason, Hamlet's character was raised and invigorated. When, now, this dignified and acute Hamlet of the lost play had received his commands from the Ghost, and was primed with his revengeful purpose, it was evident that he must be checked, or the play would end with the first two acts. Two expedients were hit upon to delay the killing of the King. The first was the question of the honesty of the Ghost, which involved the play within the play. The second was the scene where Hamlet surprises the King at his prayers. Here it is shown that, to make his filial revenge complete, he must, according to the obsolete theology of the time, kill the King

> about some act
> That has no relish of salvation in't,

because

> He took my father grossly, full of bread,
> With all his crimes broad blown, as flush as May.

The modern explanation of these truculent lines is that, with instinctive horror of bloodshed, Hamlet was practicing self-deception ; but not until Shakspere's final version, when Hamlet became so highly self-conscious and intellectual, can this explanation bear the slightest pertinence. The cruel cunning is precisely in character with the Hamblet of the *Hystorie*, and likewise with Kyd's Hieronimo in *The Spanish Tragedy*. It was doubtless highly characteristic also of the Hamlet of the lost play. Yet, even in Shakspere's first quarto, Hamlet, when he appears at his best, is gentle enough to rise above the cruelty of this revenge. His character thus bears two distinctly contradictory phases—one a remnant of the Prince of the lost play, the other a foreshadowing of the Hamlet that was to come. That Shakspere was fully aware of this double nature we need not question ; but we must also keep in mind that if he were to remove the seat of the trouble, the entire scene of the King's prayer, one of the already too few explanations of Hamlet's delay, would be sacrificed. Thus

47

the inevitable result of bringing in the Ghost was to saddle upon the Prince—eventually so gentle—one of the most diabolical sentiments the mind of man can frame.

The history of Hamlet's madness presents another case of the same kind. In all the pre-Shaksperean forms of the story there was clearly no real insanity ; and the tradition on this point was so strong that it would have been a dramatic impropriety to make Ham-*The history of Hamlet's madness.* let really mad. In the majority of the scenes of Shakspere's first quarto, consequently, there is not the slightest doubt that Hamlet is pretending the madman : the entire action of the play rests upon this fact. Under Shakspere's remodelling, however, his mind has become extremely acute and sensitive, and perhaps morbid ; and the mental strain he is under is overpowering. He has lost the cold and cunning ' subtiltie ' of the Hamblet of the *Hystorie*, and is vested with a passionate trenchancy of wit. As a result, it is not always clear that he is perfectly sane. On this point accordingly, as well as on the point of the gentleness of his spirit, Shak-

48

spere's happiest additions to the old tragedy of blood were precisely contradictory to its vital structure as a drama. Wherever Hamlet is in action his character dates back to the lost play: the Shaksperean element has to do almost exclusively with the reflective, imaginative, humane traits of his portraiture. Yet even if it ever occurred to Shakspere that the scenes where Hamlet was most highly wrought intellectually were not consonant with the scenes where he was more coldly playing the madman, it could scarcely have troubled him ; for his audience was nothing if not uncritical. In point of fact, it was two hundred years before serious doubt of Hamlet's sanity was aroused ; and even yet comparatively few students of Shakspere are convinced that he is really mad. To reconstruct the whole play so as to bring it into harmony with the refined traits lately developed in Hamlet's character would have been only less out of the question than to remove the scene where he surprised the King at his prayers. Hamlet's pretended madness caused too much mirth to the vulgar, to be dispensable from a tragedy without underplot.

The great scene with Ophelia. Hamlet's cruelty to Ophelia, however, is to be accounted for only by reference to that Elizabethan attitude toward suffering and insanity which we found in the lost play. If I can show that to Shakspere's audiences these scenes possessed an element of now-archaic comedy, many contradictory facts of the Prince's portraiture may be accounted for. In order to show this scientifically, it is necessary to ascertain the precise attitude of the Elizabethans toward those scenes in their drama in which cruelty is most evidently treated in the bear-whipping spirit, and madness after the fashion of the gallants and gentlewomen in Armin's anecdote.

IV

That no subject was too high for this archaic comedy is apparent in the Chester Miracle play of *Noah's Flood*, which was written in the latter half of the fourteenth century. It describes the difficulty Noah and his sons had in inducing his wife to embark.

GRUESOME
COMEDY IN
THE OLD
DRAMA

1.Noah's Flood.

'*Noye* . . .
Wyffe, we shall in this vessell be kepte,
My children and thou I woulde ye in lepte.

Noyes Wiffe
In fayth, Noye, I hade as leffe thou slepte!
For all thy frynishe fare,
I will not doe after thy reade.

Noye
Good Wyffe, doe nowe as I thee bydde.

Noyes Wiffe
Be Christe! not or I see more neede,
Though thou stande all daye and stare.

Noye
Lorde, that wemen be crabbed aye,
And non are meke I dare well saye;
That is well seene by me to daye,
In witnesse of you ichone.'

51

With this astute observation to the audience
Noah contents himself until the ark is finished
and all the animals are on board.

> '*Noye*
> Wiffe, come in : why standes thou their?
> Thou arte ever frowarde, I dare well sweare;
> Come in, one Godes name! halfe tyme yt
> For feare leste that we drowne.   [were,
>
> *Noyes Wiffe*
> Yea, sir, sette up youer saile,
> And rowe fourth with evill haile,
> For withouten fayle
> I will not oute of this towne ;
> But I have my gossippes everyechone,
> One foote further I will not gone : . . .
> They loven me full wel, by Christe!
> But thou lett them into thy cheiste,
> Elles rowe nowe wher thy leiste,
> And gette thee a newe wiffe.
>
> *Noye*
> Seme, sonne, loe! thy mother is wrawe ;
> Be God, such another I doe not knowe.
>
> *Sem*
> Father, I shall fetch her in, I trowe,
> Withoutten anye fayle.'

Here follows a sharp dispute, and probably a scuffle, in which Noah's wife is apparently by no means worsted. At any rate she gathers her gossips about her and sings a jolly drinking song. 'Jeffatte' remonstrates with no avail, and finally 'Sem' carries her bodily into the ark. 'Welckome, wiffe, into this botte,' says Noah. 'Have thou that for thy note!' she replies, evidently striking him as she is carried up the gang-plank. 'Ha, ha! marye, this is hotte!' Noah laughs good-naturedly. Then they all join in a genuinely pious song, the waters close in, and God ends the play with a long speech in praise of Noah. That our forefathers accepted such reverend personages in so mirthful a farce, makes it appear less improbable that they managed to get more or less fun out of Hamlet and Ophelia.

A somewhat more complex instance is presented in the tragic end of Marlowe's *Jew of Malta*, which was written and acted during Shakspere's early manhood. Barabas, the Jew, personifies the greed for gold; and, in the opening scene of the play at least, appears splendidly opulent and powerful. Still, since he is a Jew, he can only be an object of hatred and abhorrence to an Elizabethan audience. He goes through four acts doing deeds of cruelty and perfidy; and in the fifth act, as every one must expect, he is caught up with. Relying on the aid of the Governor of Malta, he is about to put an end to Calymath, traitorously, in the following manner:

2. Marlowe's 'Jew of Malta.'

> '*Bar.* . . Now as for *Calymath* and his consorts,
> Here haue I made a dainty Gallery,
> The floore whereof, this Cable being cut,
> Doth fall asunder; so that it doth sinke
> Into a deepe pit past recouery . . .
> A warning-peece shall be shot off from the Tower,
> To giue thee knowledge when to cut the cord,
> And fire the house; say, will not this be braue? . . .
> *Enter Calymath and Bashawes.* . . .
> *Bar.* Will't please thee, mighty *Selim-Calymath*,
> To ascend our homely stayres?'

54

But the Governor is not to be counted on.

'*Gov.*   Stay, *Calymath ;*
For I will shew thee greater curtesie
Than *Barabas* would haue affoorded thee.
Kni.   Sound a charge there !
[*A charge sounded within.   Ferneze cuts the cord : the floor of the gallary gives way, and Barabas falls into a caldron.*]
Bar.   Helpe, helpe me! Christians, helpe.
Fern.   See, *Calymath*, this was deuis'd
          for thee !'   *Ed.* 1633, *fol. K* 2 ; *or Act V., Sc. VI.*

This is a case of the biter bitten.   The hatred and abhorrence which Barabas has aroused earlier in the play are allayed by this bit of poetic justice ; and the piece ends in a burst of savagely triumphant mirth.   The *Jew of Malta* is the direct prototype of Shakspere's *Merchant of Venice*, which was first called the *Jew of Venice.*

Instances of the comic aspect of insanity on the Elizabethan stage are not far to seek. In Kyd's *Spanish Tragedy*, Hieronimo's son has been murdered by one Lorenzo, and Hieronimo 'runnes lunaticke' with grief and the desire for revenge.

3. *Kyd's 'Spanish Tragedy.'*

> '*Enter two Portingales, and Hieronimo
> meets them.* . . .
> *2.* You could not tell vs if his sonne were
> there ?
> *Hier.* Who, my Lord, *Lorenzo.*
> *1.* I, sir.
> *He goes in at one dore, and comes out at
> another.*
> *Hier.* . . . There, in a brazen Caldron
> fixt by *Iove,*
> In his fell wrath vpon a sulpher flame :
> Your selues shall finde *Lorenzo* bathing him,
> In boyling lead and blood of innocents.
> *1.* Ha, ha, ha.
> *Hier.* Ha, ha, ha: why ha, ha, ha.
> Forwell good ha, ha, ha. *Exit.*
> *2.* Doubtlesse this man is passing luna-
> ticke.'
>
> *Ed.* 1602, *fol. G* 3 *; Ed. Dodsley-Hazlitt, p.* 106.

Kyd's Hamlet could have been no more
above such a scene than his companion figure,
Hieronimo.

A more amusing instance is in the comic
4. Middleton's underplot of Middleton's tragedy of *The
'Changeling.' Changeling.* Alibius, 'a Doctor, who under-

takes the cure of fools and madmen,' is guarding a beautiful young wife. Antonio, 'a pretended changeling,' and Franciscus, 'a counterfeit madman,' have assumed their disguises to gain entrance to Alibius's home. The situation is roughly the same as in the comic underplot of Beaumont and Fletcher's *Spanish Curate*, where Leandro gains access to the Notary's wife, Amaranta, by becoming the notary's law pupil. In Middleton's underplot, however, the scene is in Bedlam. Fools and madmen go through their antics on the stage ; while among them the two young bucks vie with each other in simulating madness, and in assailing in the interims the mad-house keeper's wife. To give an adequate idea of the kind of comedy this produces, it would be necessary to quote the entire underplot. Roughly we have here, on the one hand, a nest of genuine ninnies, like Armin's Leonard ; and on the other, a couple of gallants pretending madness for their personal ends, like the Hamlet of the lost play. Although the tragic scenes of *The Changeling* make one of the most effective dramas outside the covers of Shakspere, this mad underplot was so popular that it usurped the title of the play.

5. *Webster's 'Duchess of Malfi.'* The madmen in the tragic climax of Webster's *Duchess of Malfi,* a play belonging to the later school of tragedies of blood, present a most difficult and complex problem The Duchess' brother, Ferdinand, has separated her violently from her husband, and is putting her to death in a darkened room, with various ingenious tortures.

'*Ferd.* . . Here's a hand,
To which you haue vow'd much loue : the
    Ring vpon't   *giues her a dead*
You gaue.   *mans hand.'*

The Duchess supposes that her husband has returned and is standing beside her.

'*Duch.* I affectionately kisse it : . . .
    You are very cold.
I feare you are not well after your trauell :
Hah ? lights : oh horrible :
Ferd. Let her haue lights enough   *Exit.'*
             Ed. 1623, *Act IIII., Scene I.*

The madmen are introduced in the next scene.

'*Servant.*   I am come to tell you,
  Your brother hath entended you some
       sport :
  A great Physitian, when the Pope was
       sicke
  Of a deepe mellancholly, presented him
  With seuerall sorts of mad-men, which
       wilde obiect
  (Being full of change, and sport,) forc'd
       him to laugh,
  And so th' impost-hume broke : the selfe
       same cure,
  The Duke intends on you. . . .
  There's a mad Lawyer, and a secular
       Priest,
  A Doctor that hath forfeited his wits
  By iealousie : an Astrologian,
  That in his workes, sayd such a day o'
       th' moneth,
  Should be the day of doome ; and,
       fayling of't,
  Ran mad : . . .'
The madmen enter. . . .

1. Come on Sir, I will lay the law to you.
2. Oh, rather lay a coraziue, the law will
eate to the bone.
3. He that drinkes but to satisfie nature
is damn'd.
4. If I had my glasse here, I would shew
a sight should make
All the women here, call me mad Doctor,
1. What's he, a rope-maker?
2. No, no, no, a snufling knaue, that
while he shewes the
Tombes, will haue his hand in a wenches
placket.
3. Woe, to the Caroach, that brought
home my wife from
The Masque, at three a clocke in the
morning, it had a large
Feather-bed in it.'   *Actus IIII., Scena II.*

After this comes the death of the Duchess—
perhaps the most brutally tremendous scene
in English literature.

Now what was the dramatic purpose of
this episode of the madmen? To the modern mind it appears just such another savage
persecution of the Duchess as the episode

of the dead man's hand. To the Duchess certainly it can be nothing else. We should have to assume that to the audience too it was simply that, except for one fact : When the madmen come in they *are* ' full of change and sport '—characteristic Elizabethan sport, which, terrible as it was supposed to be to the Duchess, could not fail to amuse the audience. The difference in the.point of view of the Duchess and of the audience is aptly illustrated by a passage in the very same play. Delio brings Julia news of her husband's approach.

'*Del.* I neuer knew man, and beast, of a
    horse, and a knight,
So weary of each other, if he had had
    a good backe,
He would haue vndertooke to haue borne
    his horse,
His breech was so pittifully sore.
Julia. *Your laughter,*
Is my pitty.'   *Actus II., Scena IIII.*

So with the Duchess. In spite of the sight of her suffering, the jests of the madmen are precisely of a nature to amuse the audience.

Consider now the dramatic situation.

The playwright is on the verge of one of the most horribly affecting scenes in literature, but the spectators have already been sated with horrors. There must be a laughing spell to rest them for what is to come, yet the playwright must not break the continuity of the climax by bringing in a purely comic scene. As Webster solves this dramatic problem, the Duchess is represented all the time in extreme torture. Nevertheless, the madmen, who are her 'pitty,' are the 'laughter' of the audience ; though doubtless the audience never entirely forgets the horror of her situation.

The general correspondence between the brutally serious side of the plays reviewed, and the brutal comedy of the scenes that were evidently intended to relieve the strain of continued tragedy, can scarcely have escaped attention ; and the reason for this correspondence is not far to seek. The tragedy of blood had an atmosphere of its own, where not only was the brutally comic in place, but where refined comedy would have been a positive fault in chiaroscuro.

The scenes I have instanced cannot be fully understood without a careful reading of the plays in which they occur. Indeed, a thorough study of this subject would carry one much farther. I have selected these few passages because they occur in the most celebrated of the old dramas. Similar ones may be found in almost any old writer. For the comic aspect of physical torture, consult the fight between Gammer Chat and Gammer Gurton in *Gammer Gurton's Needle.* The incident of Bajazeth and his cage in Marlowe's *Tamburlaine* is also suggestive. For the comic treatment of madness, consult the fifth act of Dekker's *Honest Whore.*

It is yet to be made evident that Shakspere would be guilty of the grossness of his contemporaries. The first part of *Henry IV.* will give a good instance. Prince Hal has done the last rites of chivalry over the body of his vanquished rival, Hotspur, and has left him with a speech, the pathos and ideal manhood of which are beyond praise. Yet no sooner is he off the stage than Falstaff rises from the ground where he has been shamming dead,

6. Falstaff in 'Henry IV.'

speaks twenty lines of buffoonery, stabs Hotspur's body, and finally 'takes up Hotspur on his back' and lugs him off the stage. On the next page he claims the honor of killing Hotspur. 'There is Percy,' he says to Hal, '(*throwing the body down*): if your father will do me any honor, so; if not, let him kill the next Percy himself.' The Hamlet of the first quarto could scarcely have been more sacred from this sort of fun than Hotspur.

The same sacrilege may be found in *King Lear* and in the *Merchant of Venice*. An admirable exposition of this is in Professor Barrett Wendell's lectures on Shakspere, first delivered at Harvard University in 1892–3, and since published, the brief manuscript notes of which he has kindly permitted me to quote. They give chiefly the results. The sum total of the evidence of these statements would involve an essay within the essay.

7. *'King Lear.'*   '*Lear* seems originally to have been popular. This I conceive can hardly have been for the reasons that make it perennially great. As a mere guess, I venture to suggest two grounds

64

for its popularity which would have appealed to an Elizabethan audience, and would quite fail to appeal to an audience of to-day. The first is an almost ultimate chance for sonorous rant, offered by the part of Lear; the second is the conventionally comic element which the Elizabethan audience recognized in insanity. These guesses I purposely mention and emphasize. True or false, they certainly serve to recall a true fact that we constantly lose sight of, the essential difference of Shakspere's world from ours.

'*Lear* is after all originally contemporary with the old tragedies of blood, and not twenty years removed from Tamburlaine himself.

'The title of the quarto of *Lear* emphasizes "the unfortunate life of Edgar" and "the sudden and assumed humours of Tom of Bedlam" (that is of Edgar) just as the title of the quarto of *Henry IV.* emphasizes Falstaff; and of *Henry V.*, Falstaff and Pistol. Edgar, I imagine, was really conceived by the author to be comic, to lighten the situation throughout, and as the play was popular I think the audience must have taken this view.'

An actor, now living, who took the part of Edgar in Booth's company, once assured me that in Texas, and other places remote from the centres of culture, his part was often laughed at, though he spared no effort to bring out its tragedy.

Of Shylock, Professor Wendell says :

8. 'The Merchant of Venice.'

'His . . . treatment by the very Christians he has obliged, naturally arouses all the evil in him. His revenge is wholly comprehensible—not so to me, is the contemptuous brutality with which · he finally meets.

'To understand this we must deliberately revive some dead sentiments of the world,— its ecclesiastically fostered abhorrence of usury and of Jews. Vastly foreign these data of Elizabethan England to a commercial and a sentimentally philanthropic age and people like our own. But even when we have . . . tried to put ourselves in the place of Shakspere's audiences, we have not done enough. To me, at all events, the treatment of Shylock as we conceive him now-a-days, remains, in spite of my imaginative efforts, sympathetically

66

repellant. And so, the whole effect of the play remains artistically unsatisfying. I am asked to give full sympathy to people whose conduct is ultimately outrageous. Where is the trouble? As a dramatic artist Shakspere can hardly be believed to have intended such an effect as this. Is the Hebraic Shylock of our stage really "the Jew that Shakspere drew?"

'This Hebraic Shylock is reputed to date from Macklin's performance in 1741, which Pope described in that doggerel couplet. And even Macklin dared not discard the traditional blood-red wig of the traditional Judas of the miracle plays. Before his time, so far as we can learn, the character was traditionally treated as low comedy. Clearly this old conception does not fit the lines. The character as a character is a great, serious Shaksperean creation, which may be studied and reasoned about psychologically almost like a human being. In literature, at all events, we consider rather what people are than what they seem like. In studying character we are instinctively inclined to neglect the various bodily forms in which character may mani-

67

fest itself. Is not this perhaps the trouble here?

'Elizabethan England was childishly brutal. . . . Elizabethan England held lunacy highly comic. It saw rather the grotesqueness than the horror of physical torture. Is not what so repels our sympathy, after all, not so much the inherent brutality of the treatment Shylock receives, as the application of such treatment to the kind of Shylock whom we see receive it? This is a grand Hebraic figure, smacking of the prophets. Would not a mean, cringing, "jewy" Shylock—reminding one of the pimps and pawnbrokers who to-day make up the Jewish rabble,—repel sympathy still—for all Shakspere's sympathetic psychology? Surely it would have done so in that age so foreign to our fine philanthropy—the brutally childish England of Elizabeth. And some such childish, unfeeling conception must in my opinion have been the real conception of Shakspere. As an artistic playwright, he could not have meant our sympathy to go with Shylock. No rendering of Shylock, then, that renders

68

the part essentially so noble as to be seriously sympathetic, can, in my opinion, make his fate artistically tolerable. I know of few facts that emphasize more forcibly than this the ultimate remoteness from our own world not only of Elizabethan England, but also of Shakspere, the Elizabethan playwright.'

The actual growth in Hamlet's character from Kyd's lost play to Shakspere's final version was precisely similar to the growth in the interpretation of Shylock. Even in Shakspere's time, as has been pointed out, it so far upset the balance between comedy and tragedy as to necessitate the introduction of new comic scenes in the first quarto.

Thus far I have tacitly assumed that the comic delight in physical suffering and insanity is Elizabethan, and archaic. It was distinctly characteristic of Elizabeth's England, but not exclusively so. There is abundant evidence that it existed in post-Shaksperean literature. A notable instance is Milton's description of the fate of popish sinners—'eremites and friars' in the third book of *Paradise Lost*. And in at least two

Gruesome comedy since Shakspere.

Milton.

69

modern plays extreme physical suffering—
a villain crushed under an elevator, and the
accidental application of a mustard plaster to
a bald head—has been introduced as comedy.

Modern plays,
etc.

An excellent modern instance of the delight
in madmen is to be found in Scott's *Anti-
quary;* and, though extinct on the stage, it
exists to-day among uneducated men and in
almost every robust boy. In rural districts
when idiots are at large it is by no means
uncommon to see them the friend and laughing stock of the neighbourhood, precisely as
were Armin's ninnies.

This treatment of insanity finds a very
suggestive parallel in our conventional attitude toward that temporary insanity, drunkenness. This, though we usually treat it
essentially as tragedy, we often present at

The modern
delight in
drunkenness.

first in a largely comic aspect. Examples
may be found in the novels of so late a writer
as Mr. Howells. For instance, the man who
is drunk on board the Aroostook; Bartley
Hubbard, in the *Modern Instance;* and the
scene in *Annie Kilburn* where the lawyer
Putney gets drunk. Three centuries from

now, perhaps, it will take as strong an effort of historical imagination to appreciate the fun of Putney's drunken gibes as it takes to-day to appreciate the humour of Hamlet's hoax upon Ophelia.

To recapitulate, I have shown that the *A summary.* plot of Shakspere's *Hamlet* is that of a crude tragedy of blood ; and that in the lost play upon which Shakspere worked Hamlet's madness was made comic even in the most serious scenes. I have shown, too, that such a state of affairs was quite in character with known traits of Shakspere's audience. I then showed that, owing to Shakspere's methods in writing plays, the necessities of the plot upon which he worked, and the prestige of the story, he would not, in refining *Hamlet*, be likely to make it a consistent whole ; and moreover that he would not be apt wholly to eradicate the now archaic comic treatment of Hamlet's madness. The probability of this last was strengthened by an exposition of certain scenes in the plays of Shakspere's contemporaries, and in Shakspere's own plays, where a comic treatment of suffering and madness is evident. Incidentally I have noticed that the Elizabethan attitude toward insanity is not yet extinct. It now remains to show that in Shakspere's first quarto of *Hamlet* distinct traces remain of the comic treatment of suffering and insanity.

V

Several scenes might be cited, for instance the 'Punch and Judy show at Ophelia's grave,' as one critic calls the struggle between Hamlet and Laertes; or the pathetic scene where Ophelia, in her madness, sings amusingly coarse songs. But space restricts me to the scene upon which there is most evidence—that where Hamlet appears to treat Ophelia with such contempt and cruelty. The emotions here, however we may choose to conceive them, are more complex than in any Shaksperean scene yet discussed, and, as will appear later, the archaism of this scene in the lost play is more complete; yet here, if anywhere, it will be possible to clinch my hypotheses and analogies with purely scientific evidence. Not only will the scene in itself be highly significant, but it will, I think, afford the strongest possible evidence in support of the suppositions hitherto advanced.

I have tried to prove that in the lost play the Hamlet-Ophelia scene had a comic aspect; and in the character of the many *The Hamlet-* scenes since quoted from the Elizabethan *Ophelia scene.* drama, my opinion has received strong though indirect confirmation. When now one tries to fix upon the exact spirit of the Shaksperian version of this scene according to modern conceptions, one finds that it has baffled critics and actors. Johnson and Steevens, who were nearer to Shakspere in point of time, find, as we have seen, that Hamlet is actuated by sheer cruelty; and many commentators have reiterated the charge, insisting that no skill in acting is able to remove an impression approaching to actual pain, unless by a gross violation of the text and the meaning of the author. The violation referred to consists in making Hamlet see the 'lawful espials,' and in making him wholly insane. His cruelty to Ophelia is then pardonable, one may believe, on the score of self-defense. Certain of the actors however, and notably Booth, have evidently been ill-satisfied with this feeble casuistry, for

74

they have represented Hamlet actually mad. Thus both the text and early traditions of the play go by the board. Yet this rendering makes the scene, according to an eminent writer, 'the most terrifically affecting in Shakespeare.' Now any one of these interpretations, from Dr. Johnson down, would satisfy the most exacting. But the fact that almost every commentator and actor has a view radically different from the views of all others, is far from satisfying. For myself, my sole excuse for speaking is that I do not attempt an explanation, but rather try to show that, owing to an inheritance of archaic comedy from the lost play, the facts of the scene, according to modern standards, admit of no reconcilement.

That a trace of comedy persists in the demand that Polonius 'play the foole no where but in his owne house' I have already indicated; but I have omitted to point out how capital a laugh can be made of this if we once quit *Traces of* our conventional reverence for the scene. As *comedy.* Hamlet is speaking, Polonius is peeping out from behind the arras that hangs before the

75

'study,' where he has been 'close,' and is quite sure that he is about to gain evidence for the King that Hamlet's madness springs from love. He is visible to the audience, whether or not he has been discovered by Hamlet. But instead of the love-scene, Polonius sees a most astonishing bit of satire on love, and in the end receives a slap in the face himself. A single telling grimace here from the venerable fool would be enough to set the pit howling. The comedy of this situation is distinctly stronger than that in the scene where Hamlet pretends to take Polonius for a fishmonger, because the old courtier is as a woodcock to his own springe, neatly trapped in accordance with the laws both of poetic justice and of the comedy of situation. The scene is, I take it, sufficient to prove a cousinship, however remote, between the German play and the first quarto.

The degree of such relationship cannot be *A guess as to this scene in the lost play.* calculated until we settle definitely the character of the corresponding scene in the lost play. A natural supposition is that it stood midway between the Shaksperean and the

German scenes. Still it is not easy to figure what it would be in this case, any more than to imagine what sort of beast would be cousin to the tiger and the ape. Fortunately in Webster's *Duchess of Malfi*, we have a scene that is similar enough to be significant on this point. Indeed, as Webster was in the habit of imitating Shakspere's scenes, this might be regarded as an echo of the earlier version of Hamlet's satire on women.

'*Bos.* . . You come from painting now?

Old Lady. From what?

Bos. Why, from your scuruy face-phy sicke,

To behold thee not painted enclines some what neere

A miracle: These in thy face here, were deepe rutts,

And foule sloughes the last progresse:

There was a Lady in *France*, that hauing had the small pockes,

Flead the skinne off her face, to make it more leuell;

And whereas before she look'd like a Nut-meg-grater,

77

After she resembled an abortiue hedge-
hog.

Old Lady. Doe you call this painting?

Bos. No, no, but you call carreening
of an old

Morphew'd Lady, to make her disem-
bogue againe,

There's rough-cast phrase to your plas-
tique.'   *Actus II., Scena I.*

The rest of the scene is similarly satirical,
but too coarse to quote.

This play, as we have already seen, is a
tragedy of blood, bristling with horrors, and
without comic underplot. The Old Lady appears only in this scene and one other, and
speaks in each about a score of feeble words.
Her appearance is obviously a 'fetch'; and,
considering the nature of the tragedy, not a
'fetch' to increase the horror. She typifies
the vices of women, which, even to-day, we
oftenest treat in their merely amusing aspect,
and is thus made the object of brutal satire.
When she goes out, the tragic incidents of
the play are resumed with renewed spirit. If,

now, Bosola, the villain, were saving himself from tyranny by feigned madness, and the Old Lady were a woman sent—innocently or not—to elicit his secret, a scene precisely similar to the Hamlet-Ophelia scene would result, and would afford even more legitimate sport than the scene in the *Duchess*, because the pretence of madness and the presence of the King and his Councillor in concealment would make a comic 'situation.'

Let us suppose then, for the nonce, that *Shakspere's first version of the Hamlet-Ophelia scene.* even in the first quarto the Hamlet-Ophelia scene had a distinctly comic aspect, in spite of its seriousness. To realize its precise character in this case we must put aside, first of all, the memory of the Hamlet of the familiar version, and think of the cruder Hamlet of the first quarto. Ophelia, likewise, we must conceive as a very near relative of the 'beawtifull lady' of the *Hystorie*, not as the highly discreet woman of the modern stage. We must bear in mind, too, that many features of the scene had long been familiar to Shakspere's audience, through the *Hystorie* and the lost play, in a comic form.

Let us look at two or three individual speeches. The situation of a man sailing under false colours is very common in comedy, and the blunders it occasions seldom fail to divert an audience. If, when Polonius was so thoroughly outwitted—'Let the doores be shut,' etc.—or while Ophelia was being rated for the vices of women—'Your wantonnesse . . . hath made me madde'— the audience listened with childish delight, then Ophelia's speeches 'Oh heauens secure him!' and 'Pray God restore him,' added hugely to the comedy. If, on the contrary, the Hamlet of the first quarto was so highly endowed with unbalanced intellect that he appeared to the Elizabethan audience quite unhinged, the scene might possibly have appeared, as it is with us, in the words of the prominent critic, 'the most terrifically affecting scene in Shakespeare.' The degree of comedy would probably vary according to the temperament of the spectator. Indeed, my personal opinion is, that Shakspere's audiences were quite capable of feeling strongly and simultaneously both the archaic comedy and the enduring tragedy of the scene. It has too often been necessary in the course of this essay to point out the brutality of some of their mental attitudes, and their lack of modern conventional standards in taste and feeling. How strong their natural instincts were in mirth, pathos, and terror, is evident in the fact that they made possible the marvellously varied and luxuriant Shaksperean drama. It was not without reason that Robert Armin complained of those that 'would not seeme too immodest' in expressing natural feeling; and 'thinke to make all, when God knowes they marre all.' It would perhaps be as well for the modern novel and stage if taste and emotion were more spontaneous and less a matter of critical convention.

Thus far the evidence has been, as hitherto, only partially scientific; but this is not the case with that brought to light by a comparison of the text of the German version already quoted in full (pp. 23, 24) with the text of the first quarto. The fact that there is here the closest verbal parallel

places the kinship in spirit beyond reason-
The identity of
the Shakspe-
rean with the
German
version able doubt. The only passages in the
whole German scene that are unrepresented
in Shakspere are the unimportant sentence
'get thee away . . .' and the anecdote,
which there is reason to hope saw light on
German soil. When Ophelia enters in the
German play, she says 'I pray your highness to take back the jewel which you
presented to me;' which is the counterpart
of her first speech in the first quarto, 'My
Lord, I haue sought opportunitie, which
now I haue, to redeliuer to your worthy
handes, a small remembrance, such tokens
which I haue receiued of you.' The German Hamlet says, 'What, girl! wouldst thou
have a husband? . . . Hearken, girl,
you young women do nothing but lead
young fellows astray.' Shakspere's Hamlet
says, 'But if thou wilt needes marry, marry
a foole, For wisemen know well enough,
What monsters ye make of them.' After
this the German Hamlet says, 'Your beauty
you buy of the apothecaries and peddlers,'
which in Shakspere is, 'Nay, I haue heard

of your paintings too, God hath giuen you one face, And you make your selues another.' Both scenes end with the familiar 'To a Nunnery goe.' Thus the first and last features of the scene are identical, and every intermediate speech in the German version, with the trifling exception noted, is represented in Shakspere. We have here positive proof that the two scenes—one abject buffoonery, and the other capable of appealing to the modern mind as 'the most terrifically affecting scene in Shakespeare'—were constructed on precisely the same lines. If these instances are insufficient, the reader may consult at his leisure the coarse comic treatment of Ophelia's madness in the German play, and compare it word for word with the text of this most tragic scene in Shakspere. The same verbal parallel is evident, though in a less marked degree. We must conclude that *the final proof* even in Shakspere's first version the comic *that Hamlet's madness had a* element, now quite archaic, must have been *comic aspect.* distinctly evident to the Elizabethans.

But what of the ultimate Hamlet of the Shaksperian stage? We know that in the

*Shakspere's
final version.* second quarto the distinctively Shaksperian elements of the Prince's character were added,—the philosophic and the poetic, those flashes of imagination, those deep and fine touches of a moody and cheerless yet noble philosophy. For a treatment of this I refer to the modern critics, who have rightly taken it as the characteristic and significant aspect. The speeches that we know to have come from the old play, however, were left in their places almost intact—in the Hamlet-Ophelia scene quite intact; and though we may assume that the traits last evolved in the Prince's character tended to distract attention from them, to gloss them over, they nevertheless remain to this day stubbornly inconsistent with the gentler traits of the Prince we know and love. When Hamlet is in action he is to be judged by the standards of the tragedy of blood and revenge. It is only in his speech and manner that the Shaksperian conception shines forth. In this fact lies the root of most of the disagreements among the modern critics and actors.

Yet for the modern stage all this has little *The Hamlet of* significance. Full as our Hamlet is of viola- *the modern* tions of the text, it is for us the only Hamlet. *stage.* 'In a deep embayed window Ophelia kneels.' Hamlet 'steadies himself by the balustrade, moves on again mechanically, is stopped by a chair, sinks into it,—still silent, utterly absorbed. In another moment the "To be, or not to be" is uttered in a voice at first almost inaudible. . . Rising suddenly and crossing toward the window, he sees Ophelia. His whole face changes. A lovely tenderness suffuses it. Sweetness fills his tones as he addresses her. When, with exquisite softness of manner, he draws nearer to her, he catches a glimpse of the "lawful espials" in the gallery above . . . When he says suddenly, "Where's your father?" he lays his hand upon Ophelia's head, and turns her face up to his as he stands above her. She answers, looking straight into the eyes that love her, "At home, my lord." No accusation, no reproach, could be so terrible as the sudden plucking away of his hand, and the pain of his face as he turns from her. The whole scene he plays like one distract. He is never still. He strides up and down the stage, in and out at the door, speaking outside with the same rapidity and vehemence. The speech, "I have heard of your paintings, too, well enough," he begins in the outer room, and the contemptuous words hiss as they fall. "It hath made me mad" was uttered with a flutter of the hand about the head more expressive than words. As he turned toward Ophelia for the last time, all the bitterness, all the reckless violence seemed to die out of him; his voice was full of unutterable love, of appealing tenderness, of irrevocable doom, as he uttered the last "To a nunnery go!" and tottered from the room as one who could not see for tears.'

The day for horseplay in Hamlet is manifestly past. Even to point out the birth-marks on the play would be a painful task, were not every trait of brutality so obviously outgrown. In a vastly more subtle and significant sense than that of the effusive commentators, Hamlet is 'very nature'; for though we can by no means talk of his acts as of those of 'a recently deceased acquaintance,' he still lives, *The modern* breathes, and grows in beauty. The final *Hamlet the Shaksperean* significance of the Elizabethan Hamlet is, *Hamlet.* that nature cherishes with endless loving kindness the work of those who create according to her laws, and betters them with each passing century. Every master hand that plays on a Cremona imparts a new harmony to the perfect instrument. The Cathedral softens its sharp outlines with each century that steals over it ; while every generation that treads the aisles within enriches its human associations. So with Hamlet. Each actor and critic has divined new traits of beauty, and the generations have so loved the gentleness of the Prince, that in the light of their love the brutal facts of many of the scenes in which he moves are glorified. The modern Hamlet is the real Hamlet. In the truest sense of the word he is the Shaksperean Hamlet ; and will continue so, until new ages shall add new beauties to our interpretation.

Author's Note

THE first conception of the present essay was that it should be a general study of the sources of Hamlet, with a view to clearing up, if possible, some of the literary problems of Shakspere's play. I undertook the work in the winter of 1892—3, at Harvard University, as a matter of form in taking the degree of Master of Arts with Honours in English Literature. While writing the essay I was attending *Acknowledgments.* Professor Barrett Wendell's lectures on Shakspere, published in 1894 by Charles Scribner's Sons, New York, under the title of 'William Shakspere, a Study in Elizabethan Literature.' The idea that the tragic Edgar in *Lear* is none other than the old comic Tom of Bedlam suggested that Hamlet's assumed insanity might also have had a comic aspect, at least in the pre-Shaksperean versions of the story. This idea came to me so late that the new essay it necessitated was hurried and undigested: yet it was one of the two successful theses that year in the competition for the Sohier Modern-Literature prize. During the year following it was impossible to complete my researches ; but I have lately been able to

88

do so with the aid of Malone's invaluable library, now in the Bodleian. Here, at the last moment, I came across Sarrazin's little book ' Thomas Kyd und sein Kreis,' the thoroughness and brilliancy of which need no praise of mine. The last chapter of the book gives a clear and admirable exposition of the relation-ship between the first quarto Hamlet and Kyd's old tragedy of blood, ' Der ur-Hamlet ; ' and, by showing that all which is least according to Shakspere's taste proceeded from Kyd, for the first time exonerates Shak-spere from the bizarre cruelty of many of Hamlet's deeds. My own statement of this point, however, I have decided to let stand, much though it suffers by comparison, if only to show that two students, working independently and from quite different points of view, have agreed in these important conclusions. The main point of my essay, the comic aspect of Hamlet's madness, Sarrazin has apparently not sus-pected. How much of this idea I owe to Professor Barrett Wendell must already be evident. And I am no less obliged to Professor G. L. Kittredge, of Harvard, without whose aid and encouragement I should scarcely have dared to work seriously at so extraordinary a thesis. A course of lectures on the Elizabethan Dramatists by Mr. Geo. P. Baker, also of Harvard, was of vital service. For aid in arranging and proportioning the essay I am obliged to Mr. W. D. Howells, as well as to Professors Wendell and Kittredge ; and, for a final criticism of the book as it was going through the press, to Professor F. York Powell, of Oriel College, Oxford.

Books used. The books used were chiefly the two volumes of Furness's admirable Variorum Hamlet, which contains the essential information as to all sources, texts, dates, as well as all critical and dramatic interpretations, up to the year of its publication. (J. B. Lippincott & Co., Philadelphia ; and 10, Henrietta Street, Covent Garden, London. 1877). For the old plays cited, the 'Mermaid Series of the Best Plays of the Old Dramatists' (T. Fisher Unwin, Paternoster Row, London) is perhaps most convenient, though the plays of Kyd are to be found in Dodsley's 'Old English Plays,' edited by W. C. Hazlitt (London, Reeves & Turner, 196 Strand, 1874). In my present citations I have preferred the earliest accessible quartos, and have copied accurately all imperfections of text to emphasise the remoteness of Elizabethan literature from our modern conventions of uniformity and consistency. Gregor Sarrazin's 'Thomas Kyd und sein Kreis, eine Litterarhistorische Untersuchung,' was published in Berlin by Emil Felber, in 1892. 'A Journey into England by Paul Hentzner, in the year M.D.XC.VIII.' was 'printed at Strawberry-Hill. M D CC LVII.' In modern form, it is most conveniently accessible in Cassell's National Library, London, 1889, 16°. 'A Nest of Ninnies. Simply of themselves without Compound. by Robert Armin.' was 'printed' in

AUTHOR'S NOTE

' London by T. E. for John Deane, 1608,' and in modern form is to be found in the publications of the old Shakespeare Society, London. The Chester Miracle Plays were printed by the old Shakespeare Society, London, in 1843.

J. C.

Balliol College, Oxford
Jan., 1895

Printed by R. Folkard and Son
at 22 Devonshire Street
near Queen Square
London, W.C.

91

List of Books

in

Belles Lettres

FRVCTVS INTER FOLIA

ALL THE BOOKS IN THIS CATALOGUE ARE
PUBLISHED AT NET PRICES

London: Elkin Mathews, Vigo Street, W.

1895

Telegraphic Address—
' ELEGANTIA, LONDON.'

Lector! eme, lege, et gaudebis

List of Books
IN
BELLES LETTRES
(Including some Transfers)

PUBLISHED BY

ELKIN MATHEWS

VIGO STREET, LONDON, W.

N.B.—The Authors and Publisher reserve the right of reprinting any book in this list, except in cases where a stipulation has been made to the contrary, and of printing a separate edition of any of the books for America. In the case of limited Editions, the numbers mentioned do not include the copies sent for review, nor those supplied to the public libraries.

❧§§❧

The following are a few of the Authors represented in this Catalogue:

R. D. BLACKMORE.
F. W. BOURDILLON.
BLISS CARMAN.
E. R. CHAPMAN.
ERNEST DOWSON.
MICHAEL FIELD.
T. GORDON HAKE.
ARTHUR HALLAM.
KATHARINE HINKSON.
HERBERT P. HORNE.
RICHARD HOVEY.
LEIGH HUNT.

SELWYN IMAGE.
LIONEL JOHNSON.
CHARLES LAMB.
P. B. MARSTON.
MAY PROBYN.
F. YORK POWELL.
J. A. SYMONDS.
JOHN TODHUNTER.
HENRY VAN DYKE.
FREDERICK WEDMORE.
P. H. WICKSTEED.
W. B. YEATS.

ABBOTT (DR. C. C.).

TRAVELS IN A TREE-TOP. 200 copies. Sm. 8vo. 5s. *net.*

Philadelphia : T. B. Lippincott Company.

" Dr. Abbott pleases by the interest he takes in the subject which he treats . . and he adorns his matter with a good English style . . . Altogether, with its dainty printing, it would be a charming book to read in the open air on a bright summer's day —*Athenæum*.

" He has an observant eye, a warm sympathy, and a pen that enables us to see with him. Nothing could be more restful than to read the thoughts of such nature-lovers. The very titles of his chapters suggest quiet and gentle things."—*Dublin Herald*.

THE BIRDS ABOUT US. 73 Engravings. Second Edition. Thick cr. 8vo. 5s. 6d. *net.*

Philadelphia : T. B. Lippincott Company.

BINYON (LAURENCE).

LYRIC POEMS, with title page by SELWYN IMAGE. Sq. 16mo. 5s. *net.*

"This little volume of LYRIC POEMS displays a grace of fancy, a spontaneity and individuality of inspiration, and a felicitous command of metre and diction, which lift the writer above the average of the minor singers of our time. . . . We may expect much from the writer of ' An April Day,' or of the strong concluding lines on the present age from a piece entitled ' Present and Future.' "—*Times*.

" The product of a definite and sympathetic personality."—*Globe*.

BLACKMORE (R. D.)

FRINGILLA : OR, SOME TALES IN VERSE. By the Author of "Lorna Doone." With Illustrations by LOUIS FAIRFAX-MUCKLEY and JAMES W. R. LINTON. Crown 8vo. *net.*

(Quorsum haec ? Non potui qualem Philomela querelam ; sed fringilla velut pipitabunda, vagor.)

BOURDILLON (F. W.).

A LOST GOD : a Poem in Three Books. With illustrations by H. J. FORD. Printed at the CHISWICK PRESS. 500 copies. 8vo. 6s. *net.* [*Very few remain.* Also 50 copies, royal 8vo., L. P. 17s. 6d. *net.*

" Mr. Elkin Mathews sends in a beautiful form a really striking Poem, ' A Lost God," by Mr. F. W. Bourdillon . . . . written in blank verse of much beauty and force. . . . Three full-page illustrations by Mr. H. J. Ford, curiously like old copper-plates, add further charm to the book. Deliciously idyllic is the picture of Hero and Leander, sitting in colloquy on the grass-browed rocks above the Ionian Sea, and ' The Calvary,' is as dark and strong as the other is gracious and blossoming. ' LOGROLLER, in *Star*.

" A graceful presentation in blank verse, with slight but effective dramatic setting, of the legend of the death of Pan on the morning that Christ began his teaching. '— *Times*.

[Isham Facsimile Reprint.]

BRETON (NICHOLAS).

NO WHIPPINGE, NOR TRIPPINGE, BUT A KINDE FRIENDLY SNIPPINGE. London, 1601. A Facsimile Reprint, with the original Borders to every page, with a Bibliographical Note by CHARLES EDMONDS. 200 copies, printed on hand-made paper at the CHISWICK PRESS. 12mo.   *net.*

Also 50 copies Large Paper.   *net.*

Facsimile reprint from the semi-unique copy discovered in the autumn of 1867 by Mr. Charles Edmonds in a disused lumber room at Lamport Hall, Northants (Sir Charles E. Isham's), and purchased lately by the British Museum authorities. When Dr. A. B. Grosart collected Breton's Works a few years ago for his " Chertsey Worthies Library." he was forced to confess that certain of Breton's most coveted books were missing and absolutely unavailable. The semi-unique example under notice was one of these.

CARMAN (BLISS) & RICHARD HOVEY.

SONGS FROM VAGABONDIA. With Decorations by TOM B. METEYARD. Fcap. 8vo.   *net.*

Boston: Copeland & Day.

" The Authors of the small joint volume called ' Songs from Vagabondia,' have an unmistakable right to the name of poet. These little snatches have the spirit of a gipsy Omar Khayyám. They have always careless verve, and often careless felicity ; they are masculine and rough, as roving songs should be. . . Here, certainly, is the poet's soul. . . . You have the whole spirit of the book in such an unforgetable little lyric as ' In the House of Idiedaily.' . . We refer the reader to the delightful little volume itself, which comes as a welcome interlude amidst the highly wrought introspective poetry of the day.'— FRANCIS THOMPSON, in *Merry England.*

" Bliss Carman is the author of a delightful volume of verse, ' Low Tide on Grand Pré,' and Richard Hovey is the foremost of the living poets of America, with the exception, perhaps, of Bret Harte and Joaquim Miller, whose names are more familiar. He sounds a deeper note than either of these, and deals with loftier themes."—*Dublin Express.*

" Delightful, indeed, is such singing as this, and it must be a stubborn nature that can refuse to yield to the charm of *Marna.* '— *New York Sun.*

" Plenty of sparkle, plenty of freshness, and a full measure of wholesome vigour."— R. H. STODDARD, in *New York Mail and Express.*

CHAPMAN (ELIZABETH RACHEL).

A LITTLE CHILD'S WREATH : A Sonnet Sequence. With title page and cover designed by SELWYN IMAGE. Second Edition. Sq. 16mo., green buckram. 3s. 6d. *net.*

New York: Dodd, Mead & Company.

" Contains many tender and pathetic passages, and some really exquisite and subtle touches of childhood nature. . . . The average excellence of the sonnets is undoubted."—*Spectator.*

" In these forty pages of poetry . . . we have a contribution inspired by grief for the loss of a child of seven, which is not unworthy to take its place even

CHAPMAN (ELIZABETH RACHEL)—continued.

beside 'In Memoriam.' . . . Miss Chapman has ventured upon sacred ground, but she has come off safely, with the inspiration of a divine sympathy in her soul, and with lips touched with the live coal from the altar on which glows the flame of immortal love "—W. T. STEAD, in *The Review of Reviews.*

"Full of a very solemn and beautiful but never exaggerated sentiment."— LOGROLLER, in *Star.*

"While they are brimming with tenderness and tears, they are marked with the skilled workmanship of the real po t."—*Glasgow Herald.*

"Evidently describes very real and intense sorrow. Its strains of tender sympathy will appeal specially to those whose hearts have been wrung by the loss of a young child, and the verses are touching in their simplicity."—*Morning Post.*

"Re-assures us on its first page by its sanity and its simple tenderness."—*Bookman.*

COLERIDGE (HON. STEPHEN).

THE SANCTITY OF CONFESSION: A Romance. 2nd edition. Printed by CLOWES & SON. 250 copies. Cr. 8vo. 3s. net   [*Very few remain.*

"Mr. Stephen Coleridge's sixteenth-century romance is well and pleasantly written. The style is throughout in keeping with the story; and we should imagine that t e historical probabilities are we'l observed."—*Pall Mall Gazette.*

Mr. GLADSTONE writes;—"I have read the singularly well told story. . . . It opens up questions both deep and dark; it cannot be right to accept in religion or anything else a secret which destroys the life of an innocent fellow creatue."

CORBIN (JOHN).

THE ELIZABETHAN HAMLET: A Study of the Sources, and of Shakspere's Environment, to show that the Mad Scenes had a Comic Aspect now Ignored. With a Prefatory Note by F. YORK POWELL, Professor of Modern History at the University of Oxford. Small 4to. 3s 6d. net.

New York: Charles Scribner's Sons.

"Mr. Elkin Mathews will this spring publish another addition to Shakespearean literature under the title 'The Elizabethan 'Hamlet.'' The author is Mr. John Corbin, of Balliol College, Oxford, and the volume will have an introductory note by Professor York Powell. The book is a study of the sources of 'Hamlet,' and of Shakespeare's environment, with the object of showing that the mad scenes in the play had a comic aspect now ignored Mr. Corbin's general standpoint is that Shakespeare naturally wrote the drama for Elizabethan audiences. They in their time saw jest in what would seem to us only the severest tragedy. What he wishes to get at is the comedy in 'Hamlet' according to the Elizabethan point of view."

CROSSING (WILLIAM).

THE ANCIENT CROSSES OF DARTMOOR; with a Description of their Surroundings. With 11 plates. 8vo. cloth. 4s. 6d. net.   [*Very few remain.*

DAVIES (R. R.).

> SOME ACCOUNT OF THE OLD CHURCH AT CHELSEA AND.
> OF ITS MONUMENTS.   [*In preparation.*

DE GRUCHY (AUGUSTA).

> UNDER THE HAWTHORN, AND OTHER VERSES. With
> Frontispiece by WALTER CRANE. Printed at the
> RUGBY PRESS. 300 copies. Cr. 8vo. 5s. *net.*
> Also 30 copies on Japanese vellum. 15s. *net.*

" Melodious in metre, graceful in fancy, and not without spontaneity of inspiration."—*Times.*

" Very tender and melodious is much of Mrs. De Gruchy's verse. Rare imaginative
power marks the dramatic monologue ' In the Prison Van.' "—*Speaker.*

" Distinguished by the attractive qualities of grace and refinement, and a purity
of style that is as refreshing as a limpid stream in the heat of a summer's noon. . . .
The charm of these poems lies in their naturalness, which is indeed an admirable
quality iu song."—*Saturday Review.*

DESTRÉE (OLIVIER GEORGES).

> POÈMES SANS RIMES. Imprimé à Londres aux Presses de
> Chiswick, d'apres les dessins de HERBERT P. HORNE.
> 25 copies for sale. Square cr. 8vo. 8s. 6d. *net.*

DIVERSI COLORES SERIES.

> *See* HORNE.

DOWSON (ERNEST).

> DILEMMAS : Stories and Studies in Sentiment. (A Case of
> Conscience.- The Diary of a Successful Man.—An
> Orchestral Violin.—The Statute of Limitations.—
> Souvenirs of an Egoist). Crown 8vo. 3s. 6d, *net.*
>   [*In rapid preparation.*

> POEMS (*Diversi Colores* Series). With a title design by
> H. P. HORNE. Printed at the CHISWICK PRESS, on
> hand-made paper. 16mo. 5s. *net.*   [*Shortly.*

" Mr. Dowson's contributions to the two series of the *Rhymer's Book* were
subtle and exquisite poems. He has a touch of Elizabethan distinction. . . .
Mr. Dowson's stories are very remarkable in quality."—*Boston Literary World.*

FIELD (MICHAEL).

SIGHT AND SONG (Poems on Pictures). Printed by CONSTABLES. 400 copies. 12mo. 5s. net.

[Very few remain.

"This is a fascinating little volume; one that will give to many readers a new interest in the examples of pictorial art with which it deals. Certainly, in the delight in the beauty of the human form, and of the fair shows of earth, and sea, and sky which it manifests, and in the harmonious verbal expression which this delight has found, the book is one of the most Keats-like things that has been produced since Keats himself took his seat among the immortals."—*Academy.*

"The verses have a sober grace and harmony, and the truth and poetic delicacy of the work is only realised on a close comparison with the picture itself. It is soothing and pleasant to participate in such leisurely degustation and enjoyment, such insistent penetration, for these poems are far removed from mere description, and the renderings, though somewhat lacking in the sense of humour, show both courage and poetical imagination."—*Westminster Review.*

STEPHANIA: A TRIALOGUE IN THREE ACTS. Frontispiece, colophon, and ornament for binding designed by SELWYN IMAGE. Printed by FOLKARD & SON. 250 copies (200 for sale). Pott 4to. 6s. net.

[Very few remain.

"We have true drama in 'Stephania.' . . . . Stephania, Otho, and Sylvester II., the three persons of the play, are more than mere names. . . . . Besides great effort, commendable effort, there is real greatness in this play; and the blank verse is often sinewy and strong with thought and passion."—*Speaker.*

"'Stephania' is striking in design and powerful in execution. It is a highly dramatic 'trialogue' between the Emperor Otho III , his tutor Gerbert, and Stephania, the widow of the murdered Roman Consul, Crescentius. The poem contains much fine work, and is picturesque and of poetical accent. . . ."—*Westminster Review.*

A QUESTION OF MEMORY: A PLAY IN FOUR ACTS. 100 copies only. 8vo. 5s. net. *[Very few remain.*

GALTON (ARTHUR).

ESSAYS UPON MATTHEW ARNOLD (*Diversi Colores* Series). Printed at the CHISWICK PRESS on hand-made paper. Cr. 8vo. 5s. net. *[Shortly.*

HAKE (DR. T. GORDON, "The Parable Poet.")

MADELINE, AND OTHER POEMS. Crown 8vo. 5s. net.
Transferred to the present Publisher.

"The ministry of the angel Daphne to her erring human sister is frequently related in strains of pure and elevated tenderness. Nor does the poet who can show so much delicacy fail in strength. The description of Madeline as she passes in trance to her vengeance is full of vivid pictures and charged with tragic feeling.

HAKE (DR. T. GORDON)—continued.

The individuality of the writer lies in his deep sympathy with whatever affects the being and condition of man. . . . Taken as a whole, the book has high and unusual claims."—*Athenæum.*

. " I have been reading ' Madeline ' again. For sheer originality, both of conception and of treatment, I consider that it stands alone."—MR. THEODORE WATTS.

> PARABLES AND TALES. (Mother and Child.—The Crip-
> ple.—The Blind Boy.—Old Morality.—Old Souls.—
> The Lily of the Valley.—The Deadly Nightshade.—
> The Poet). With 9 illustrations by ARTHUR HUGHES.
> Crown 8vo.   3s. 6d. net.

> *Transferred to the present Publisher.*

" The qualities of Dr. Gordon Hake's work were from the first fully admitted and warmly praised by one of the greatest of contemporary poets, who was also a critic of exceptional acuteness—Rossetti. Indeed, the only two review articles which Rossetti ever wrote were written on two of Dr. Hake's books: ' Madeline,' which he reviewed in the *Academy* in 1871, and ' Parables and Tales,' which he reviewed in the *Fortnightly* in 1873. Many eminent critics have expressed a decided preference for ' Parables and Tales' to Dr. Hake's other works, and it had the advantage of being enriched with the admirable illustrations of Arthur Hughes."—*Saturday Review,* January, 1895.

" The piece called ' Old Souls' is probably secure of a distinct place in the liter-ature of our day, and we believe the same may be predicted of other poems in the little collection just issued. . . . Should Dr. Hake's more restricted, but lovely and sincere contributions to the poetry of real life not find the immediate response they deserve, he may at least remember that others also have failed to meet at once with full justice and recognition. But we will hope for good encouragement to his present and future work; and can at least ensure the lover of poetry that in these simple pages he shall find not seldom a humanity limpid and pellucid—the well-spring of a true heart, with which his tears must mingle as with their own element.

" Dr. Hake has been fortunate in the beautiful drawings which Mr. Arthur Hughes has contributed to his little volume. No poet could have a more congenial yoke-fellow than this gifted and imaginative artist."—D. G. ROSSETTI, in the *Fortnightly.* 1873.

HALLAM (ARTHUR).

> THE POEMS OF ARTHUR HENRY HALLAM, together with
> his Essay " ON SOME OF THE CHARACTERISTICS OF
> MODERN POETRY, AND ON THE LYRICAL POEMS OF
> ALFRED TENNYSON," reprinted from the *Englishman's
> Magazine,* 1831, edited, with an introduction, by
> RICHARD LE GALLIENNE.   550 copies (500 for sale).
> Small 8vo.   5s. net.
> Also 50 copies L.P., 12s. 6d. net.

> *New York: Macmillan & Co.*

Many of these Poems are of great Tennysonian interest, having been addressed to Alfred, Charles, and Emily Tennyson.

HAMILTON (COL. IAN).

THE BALLAD OF HADJI, AND OTHER POEMS. With etched frontispiece by WILLIAM STRANG. Printed at the CHISWICK PRESS. 550 copies. 12mo. 3s. net.

Transferred by the Author to the present Publisher.

" Here is a dainty volume of clear, sparkling verse. The thought is sparkling, and the lines limpid and lightly flowing."—*Scotsman.*

" There are some pretty things in this little book."—*Spectator.*

" An unusual amount of genuine poetry is to be found in the Ballad of Hadji. The opening piece is a really fine ballad with great power, and pathos so intense as to be almost painful."—*Graphic.*

" Mr. Ian Hamilton's Ballad of Hadji is undeniably clever."—*Pall Mall Gazette.*

" The ' Ballad of Hadji' is very good, and, were it only for that, the book is well worth buying. It possesses, however, yet another strong attraction in the shape of many fantastically beautiful head and tail pieces from the pen of Mr. J. B. Clark, which are scattered throughout the volume with excellent decorative effect. '—*Chronicle.*

HARPER (CHARLES G.)

REVOLTED WOMAN : PAST, PRESENT, AND TO COME. Printed by STRANGEWAYS. Illustrated with numerous original drawings and facsimiles by the Author. Crown 8vo. 5s. net.

" Mr. Harper, like a modern John Knox, denounces the monstrous regiment of women, making the ' New Woman' the text of a discourse that bristles with historical instances and present day portraits."—*Saturday Review.*

" The illustrations are distinctly clever."—*Publishers' Circular.*

HEMINGWAY (PERCY).

OUT OF EGYPT : Stories from the Threshold of the East. Cover design by GLEESON WHITE. Crown 8vo. 3s. 6d. net.

" This is a strong book."—*Academy.*

" This is a remarkable book. Egyptian life has seldom been portrayed from the inside. . . . The author's knowledge of Arabic, his sympathy with the religion of Islam, above all his entire freedom from Western prejudice, have enabled him to learn more of what modern Egypt really is than the average Englishman could possibly acquire in a lifetime at Cairo or Port Said."—*African Review.*

" A lively and picturesque style. . . . undoubted talent."—*Manchester Guardian.*

" But seldom that the first production of an author is so mature and so finished in style as this. . . . The sketches are veritable spoils of the Egyptians—gems of prose in a setting of clear air, sharp outlines, and wondrous skies.—*Morning Leader.*

" This book places its author amongst those writers from whom lasting work of high aim is to be expected."—*The Star.*

" The tale . . . is treated with daring directness. . . An impressive and pathetic close to a story told throughout with arresting strength and simplicity "—*Daily News.*

HEMINGWAY (PERCY)—continued.

THE HAPPY-WANDERER (Poems).   With title design by
Charles I. ffoulkes.   Printed at the CHISWICK PRESS,
on hand-made paper. Sq. 16mo. 5s. *net.* [*Immediately.*

HICKEY (EMILY H.).

VERSE TALES, LYRICS AND TRANSLATIONS.   Printed at
the ARNOLD PRESS. 300 copies. Imp. 16mo. 5s. *net.*
[*Very few remain.*

'Miss Hickey's 'Verse Tales, Lyrics, and Translations' almost invariably
reach a high level of finish and completeness. The book is a string of little rounded
pearls.—*Athenæum.*

HINKSON (HENRY A.).

DUBLIN VERSES.   By MEMBERS OF TRINITY COLLEGE.
Selected and Edited by H. A. HINKSON, late Scholar
of Trinity College, Dublin.   Pott 4to.   5s. *net.*

Dublin : Hodges, Figgis & Co., Limited.

Includes contributions by the following :—Aubrey de Vere,
Sir Stephen de Vere, Oscar Wilde, J. K. Ingram, A. P. Graves,
J. Todhunter, W. E. H. Lecky, T. W. Rolleston, Edward
Dowden, G. A. Greene, Savage-Armstrong, Douglas Hyde,
R. Y. Tyrrell, G. N. Plunkett, W. Macknish Dixon, William
Wilkins, George Wilkins, and Edwin Hamilton.

HINKSON (KATHARINE).

SLOES ON THE BLACKTHORN : A VOLUME OF IRISH
STORIES.   Crown 8vo., 3s. 6d. *net.*   [*In preparation.*
LOUISE DE LA VALLIERE, AND OTHER POEMS.   Small
cr. 8vo.   3s. 6d. *net.*   [*Very few remain.*

Transferred by the Author to the present Publisher.

"Sweet, pure, and high poetry."—*Truth.*

"Very seldom is it our good fortune to close a volume of poems with such an
almost unalloyed sense of pleasure and gratitude to the author."—*Graphic.*

" HOBBY HORSE (THE)."

AN ILLUSTRATED ART MISCELLANY.   Edited by HERBERT
P. HORNE.   The Fourth Number of the New Series
will shortly appear, after which MR. MATHEWS will
publish all the numbers in a volume, price £1. 1s. *net.*
Boston : Copeland & Day.

HORNE (HERBERT P.)

DIVERSI COLORES: Poems. Vignette, &c, designed by the Author. Printed at the CHISWICK PRESS. 250 copies. 16mo. 5s. net.

Transferred by the Author to the present Publisher.

" In these few poems Mr. Horne has set before a tasteless age, and an extravagant age, examples of poetry which, without fear or hesitation, we consider to be of true and pure beauty."—*Anti-Jacobin.*

" With all his fondness for sixteenth century styles and themes, Mr. Horne is yet sufficiently individual in his thought and manner. Much of his sentiment is quite latter-day in tone and rendering ; he is a child of his time."—*Globe.*

" Mr. Horne's work is almost always carefully felicitous and may be compared with beautiful filagree work in verse. He is fully, perhaps too fully, conscious of the value of restraint, and is certainly in need of no more culture in the handling of verse —of such verse as alone he cares to work in. He has already the merits of a finished artist—or, at all events, of an artist who is capable of the utmost finish."—*Pall Mall Gazette.*

The SERIES OF BOOKS begun in "DIVERSI COLORES" by Mr. HERBERT P. HORNE, will continue to be published by Mr. Elkin Mathews.

The intention of the series is to give, in a collected and sometimes revised form, Poems and Essays by various writers, whose names have hitherto been chiefly associated with the *Hobby Horse.* The series will be edited by Mr. HERBERT P. Horne, and will contain :

No. II. POEMS AND CAROLS. By SELWYN IMAGE.
[*Just published.*

No. III. ESSAYS UPON MATTHEW ARNOLD. By ARTHUR GALTON.

No. IV. POEMS. By ERNEST DOWSON.

No. V. THE LETTERS AND PAPERS OF ADAM LEGENDRE.

Each volume will contain a new title-page and ornaments designed by the Editor ; and the volumes of verse will be uniform with "Diversi Colores."

HORTON (ALICE).

POEMS. [*Shortly.*

HUEFFER (OLIVER F. MADOX).

SONNETS AND POEMS. With a frontispiece. [*Shortly.*

HUGHES (ARTHUR).
    See HAKE.

HUNT (LEIGH).
    A VOLUME OF ESSAYS now collected for the first time.
    Edited with a critical Introduction by JOHNSON
    MONTAGU.   [In the press.

IMAGE (SELWYN).
    POEMS AND CAROLS. (Diversi Colores Series.—New
    Volume). Title design by H. P. HORNE. Printed
    on hand-made paper at the CHISWICK PRESS. 16mo.
    5s. net.   [Just ready.

    " Among the artists who have turned poets will shortly have to be reckoned Mr.
Selwyn Image. A volume of poems from his pen will be published by Mr. Elkin
Mathews before long. Those who are acquainted with Mr. Selwyn Image's work
will expect to find a real and deep poetic charm in this book."—Daily Chronicle.
    " No one else could have done it (i.e., written ' Poems and Carols ') in just this
way, and the artist himself could have done it in no other way." " A remarkable
impress of personality, and this personality of singular rarity and interest. Every
piece is perfectly composed; the ' mental cartooning,' to use Rossetti's phrase, has
been adequately done . . . an air of grave and homely order . . . a union of
quaint and subtly simple homeliness, with a somewhat abstract severity. . . . It
is a new thing, the revelation of a new poet. . . . Here is a book which may be
trusted to outlive most contemporary literature." —Saturday Review.
    " An intensely personal expression of a personality of singular charm, gravity,
fancifulness, and interest; work which is alone among contemporary verse alike in
regard to substance and to form . . . comes with more true novelty than any
book of verse published in England for some years."—Athenæum.
    " Some men seem to avoid fame as sedulously as the majority seek it. Mr. Selwyn
Image is one of these. He has achieved a charming fame by his very shyness and
mystery. His very name has a look of having been designed by the Century Guild,
and it was certainly first published in The Century Guild Hobby Horse."—The Realm.
    " In the tiny little volume of verse, ' Poems and Carols,' by Selwyn Image,
we discern a note of spontaneous inspiration, a delicate and graceful fancy, and
considerable, but unequal, skill of versification. The Carols are skilful reproductions
of that rather archaic form of composition, devotional in tone and felicitous in
sentiment. Love and nature are the principal themes of the Poems. It is difficult
not to be hackneyed in the treatment of such themes, but Mr. Image successfully
overcomes the difficulty."—The Times.
    " The Catholic movement in literature, a strong reality to-day in England as in
France, if working within narrow limits, has its newest interpretation in Mr. Selwyn
Image's ' Poems and Carols.' Of course the book is charming to look at and to
handle, since it is his. The Chiswick Press and Mr. Mathews have helped him to
realize his design."—The Sketch.

ISHAM FACSIMILE REPRINTS; Nos. III. and IV.
    See BRETON and SOUTHWELL.

    ₊ New Elizabethan Literature at the British Museum, see
The Times, 31 August, 1894, also Notes and Queries, Sept., 1894.

JACOBI (C. T.).

ON THE MAKING AND ISSUING OF BOOKS. With Numerous Ornaments. Fcap. 8vo. 2s. 6d. net. [*All sold.*.

SOME NOTES ON BOOKS AND PRINTING: a Guide for Authors and Others. 8vo. 5s. net.

[By the Author of *The Art of Thomas Hardy*].

JOHNSON (LIONEL).

POEMS. With a title design and colophon by H. P. HORNE. Printed at the CHISWICK PRESS, on hand-made paper. Sq. post 8vo. 5s. net.

Also, 25 special copies at 15s. net.

Boston : Copeland and Day.

"Mr Elkin Mathews announces some books of interest. One is a volume of poems by Mr. Lionel Johnson, who has the making of a great critic. One can always pick out his reviews in a London daily by their sanity, clear sight, and high-mindedness, as well as by the learning which unobtrusively runs like a golden thread through them. His poems have the same lofty quality, and stand out in a time when the minor muse amongst us is sick and morbid."—*Boston Literary World.*

JOHNSON (EFFIE).

IN THE FIRE, AND OTHER FANCIES. With frontispiece by WALTER CRANE. Imperial 16mo. 3s. 6d. net.

LAMB (CHARLES).

BEAUTY AND THE BEAST. With an Introduction by ANDREW LANG. Facsimile Reprint of the rare First Edition. *With 8 choice stipple engravings in brown ink, after the original plates.* Royal 16mo. 3s. 6d. net.. *Transferred to the present Publisher.*

LANG (ANDREW).

See LAMB.

LETTERS TO LIVING ARTISTS.

Fcap. 8vo. 3s. 6d. net.

LYNCH (ARTHUR).

RELIGIO ATHLETÆ. [*In preparation.*

MARSON (REV. C. L.).

A VOLUME OF SHORT STORIES.   [*In preparation.*

MARSTON (PHILIP BOURKE).

A LAST HARVEST: LYRICS AND SONNETS FROM THE
BOOK OF LOVE. Edited, with Biographical Sketch,
by LOUISE CHANDLER MOULTON. 500 copies. Printed
by MILLER & SON. Post 8vo. 5*s. net.*
                                [*Very few remain.*

Also 50 copies on hand-made L.P. 10*s.* 6*d. net.*
                                [*Very few remain.*

"Among the sonnets with which the volume concludes, there are some fine
examples of a form of verse in which all competent authorities allow that Marston
excelled 'The Breadth and Beauty of the Spacious Night,' 'To All in Haven,'
'Friendship and Love,' 'Love's Deserted Palace'—these, to mention no others,
have the 'high seriousness' which Matthew Arnold made the test of true poetry."—
Athenæum.

"Mrs. Chandler Moulton's biography is a beautiful piece of writing, and her
estimate of his work—a high estimate—is also a just one."—*Black and White.*

MASON (A. E. W.).

. . . . . .: A TALE.   [*Shortly.*

MUSA CATHOLICA.

Selected and Edited by MRS. WILLIAM SHARP.
                                [*In preparation.*

MURRAY (ALMA).

PORTRAIT AS BEATRICE CENCI. With Critical Notice
containing Four Letters from ROBERT BROWNING.
8vo. 2*s. net.*

NOEL (HON. RODEN).

POOR PEOPLE'S CHRISTMAS. Printed at the AYLESBURY
PRESS. 250 copies. 16mo. 1*s. net.*
                                [*Very few remain.*

"Displays the author at his best. . . . . Mr. Noel always has something
to say worth saying, and his technique—though like Browning, he is too intent upon
idea to bestow all due care upon form—is generally sufficient and sometimes
masterly. We hear too seldom from a poet of such deep and kindly sympathy."—
Sunday Times.

O'SULLIVAN (VINCENT).

POEMS.   [*In preparation.*

PINKERTON (PERCY).

GALEAZZO : a Venetian Episode, and other Poems. With an Etched Frontispiece. 16mo. 5s. *net.*
[*Very few remain.*
Transferred by the Author to the present Publisher.

"This little book has individuality, the mark of a true poet, of a finely-gifted nature."—MR. JOHN ADDINGTON SYMONDS, in the *Academy*.

"It is but a pamphlet stitched in a white cover. Moreover, the book is almost wholly concerned with Venice. This seems poor matter for poems ; and yet there is great charm and skill in Mr. Pinkerton's landscapes in rhyme. They are the most pleasant metrical impressions from nature one has seen for a long time."—MR. ANDREW LANG, in *Longman's Magazine*.

POWELL (F. YORK).
See CORBIN.

PROBYN (MAY).

PANSIES : A BOOK OF POEMS. With a title-page and cover design by MINNIE MATHEWS. Fcap. 8vo. 3s. 6d. *net.*

"De mon jardin, voyageur,
Vous me demandez une fleur?
Cueillez toujours—mais je n'ai,
Voyageur, que des pensées."

"Miss Probyn's earlier volumes ' Poems,' and ' A Ballad of the Road,' were published in 1881 and 1883. They attracted considerable attention, but have been long out of print. Miss Probyn did not follow them up with other volumes, and except in magazines and anthologies, she has been silent for the last ten years. In a review of ' Poems ' the *Saturday Review* said it displayed "much brightness of fancy, united with excellent metrical science;" and *The Scotsman* pronounced it to be "full of dainty charm, tender pathos, and true poetic quality." Miss Probyn is a convert to Catholicism, and her new book will contain some fervent religious poetry, often tinged with mediæval mannerism. Her carols might have been written by some very devout and simple monk of the middle ages.

RHYMERS' CLUB, THE SECOND BOOK OF THE.

Contributions by E. DOWSON, E. J. ELLIS, G. A. GREENE, A. HILLIER, LIONEL JOHNSON, RICHARD LE GALLIENNE, VICTOR PLARR, E. RADFORD, E. RHYS, T. W. ROLLESTONE, ARTHUR SYMONS, J. TODHUNTER, W. B. YEATS. Printed by MILLER & SON. 500 copies (of which 400 are for sale). 16mo. 5s. *net.*
50 copies on hand-made L.P. 10s. 6d. *net.*

New York : Dodd, Mead & Co.

"The work of twelve very competent verse writers, many of them not unknown to fame. This form of publication is not a new departure exactly, but it is a recurrence to the excellent fashion of the Elizabethan age, when ' England's Helicon,'

RHYMERS' CLUB, SECOND BOOK OF THE—continued.

Davison's ' Poetical Rhapsody,' and ' Phœnix Nest,' with scores of other collections, contained the best songs of the best song-writers of that tuneful epoch."—*Black and White.*

"The future of these thirteen writers, who have thus banded themselves together, will be watched with interest. Already there is fulfilment in their work, and there is much promise." *Speaker.*

"In the intervals of Welsh rarebit and stout provided for them at the ' Cheshire Cheese,' in Fleet Street, the members of the Rhymers' Club have produced some very pretty poems, which Mr. Elkin Mathews has issued in his notoriously dainty manner."—*Pall Mall Gazette.*

ROTHENSTEIN (WILL).

OCCASIONAL PORTRAITS. With comments on the Personages by various writers.   [*In preparation.*

SCHAFF (DR. P.).

LITERATURE AND POETRY: Papers on Dante, Latin Hymns, &c. Portrait and Plates. 100 copies only. 8vo. 10*s. net.*   [*Very few remain.*

SCULL (W. D.).

THE GARDEN OF THE MATCHBOXES, and other Stories. Crown 8vo. 3*s.* 6*d. net.*   [*In preparation.*

STRANGE (E. F.)

A BOOK OF THOUGHTS.   [*In preparation.*

[Isham Facsimile Reprint].

S[OUTHWELL] (R[OBERT]).

A FOVREFOVLD MEDITATION, OF THE FOURE LAST THINGS. COMPOSED IN A DIUINE POEME. By R. S. The author of S. Peter's complaint. London, 1606. A Facsimile Reprint, with a Bibliographical Note by CHARLES EDMONDS. 150 copies. Printed on hand-made paper at the CHISWICK PRESS. Roy. 16mo. *net.*

Also 50 copies, large paper.   *net.*

Facsimile reprint from the unique fragment discovered in the autumn of 1867 by Mr. Charles Edmonds in a disused lumber room at Lamport Hall, Northants, and lately purchased by the British Museum authorities. This fragment supplies the first sheet of a previously unknown poem by Robert Southwell, the Roman Catholic poet, whose religious fervour lends a pathetic beauty to everything that he wrote and future editors of Southwell's works will find it necessary to give it close study. The whole of the Poem has been completed from two MS. copies, which differ in the number of Stanzas.

SYMONDS (JOHN ADDINGTON).

IN THE KEY OF BLUE, AND OTHER PROSE ESSAYS.
With cover designed by C. S. RICKETTS. Printed at
the BALLANTYNE PRESS. Second Edition. Thick
cr. 8vo. 8s. 6d. net.

New York : Macmillan & Co.

"The variety of Mr. Symonds' interests! Here are criticisms upon the Venetian
Tiepolo, upon M. Zola, upon Mediæval Norman Songs, upon Elizabethan lyrics,
upon Plato's and Dante's ideals of love; and not a sign anywhere, except may be in
the last, that he has more concern for, or knowledge of, one theme than another.
Add to these artistic themes the delighted records of English or Italian scenes, with
their rich beauties of nature or of art, and the human passions that inform them.
How joyous a sense of great possessions won at no man's hurt or loss must such a
man retain."—*Daily Chronicle.*

"Some of the essays are very charming, in Mr. Symonds best style, but the
first one, that which gives its name to the volume, is at least the most curious of the
lot.'—*Speaker.*

"The other essays are the work of a sound and sensible critic."—*National
Observer.*

"The literary essays are more restrained, and the prepared student will find them
full of illumination and charm, while the descriptive papers have the attractiveness
which Mr. Symonds always gives to work in this genre."—MR. JAS. ASHCROFT
NOBLE, in *The Literary World.*

TENNYSON (LORD).

See HALLAM,—VAN DYKE.

TODHUNTER (DR. JOHN).

A SICILIAN IDYLL. With a Frontispiece by WALTER
CRANE. Printed at the CHISWICK PRESS. 250 copies.
Imp. 16mo. 5s. net. 50 copies hand-made L.P. Fcap.
4to. 10s. 6d net. [*Very few remain.*

"He combines his notes skilfully, and puts his own voice, so to speak, into
them, and the music that results is sweet and of a pastoral tunefulness."—*Speaker.*

"The blank verse is the true verse of pastoral, quiet and scholarly, with frequent
touches of beauty. The echoes of Theocritus and of the classics at large are modest
and felicitous."—*Anti-Jacobin.*

"A charming little pastoral play in one act. The verse is singularly graceful,
and many bright gems of wit sparkle in the dialogues."—*Literary World.*

"Well worthy of admiration for its grace and delicate finish, its clearness, and
its compactness."—*Athenæum.*

Also the following works by the same Author transferred
to the present Publisher, viz. :—LAURELLA, and other
Poems, 5s. net.—ALCESTIS, a Dramatic Poem, 4s. net.
—A STUDY OF SHELLEY, 5s. 6d. net.—FOREST SONGS,
and other Poems, 3s. net.—THE BANSHEE, 3s. net.—
HELENA IN TROAS, 2s. 6d. net.

TYNAN (KATHARINE).

　　See HINKSON.

VAN DYKE (HENRY).

　　THE POETRY OF TENNYSON.　　Third Edition, enlarged.
　　　　Cr. 8vo.　5*s.* 6*d. net.*

　　*The additions consist of a Portrait, Two Chapters, and the
　　　　Bibliography expanded.　The Laureate himself gave valuable
　　　　aid in correcting various details.*

　　　"Mr. Elkin Mathews publishes a new edition, revised and enlarged, of that
　　excellent work, 'The Poetry of Tennyson,' by Henry Van Dyke.　The additions
　　are considerable.　It is extremely interesting to go over the bibliographical notes
　　to see the contemptuous or, at best, contemptuously patronising tone of the reviewers
　　in the early thirties gradually turning to civility, to a loud chorus of applause."—
　　Anti-Jacobin.

　　　"Considered as an aid to the study of the Laureate, this labour of love merits
　　warm commendation.　Its grouping of the poems, its bibliography and chronology,
　　its catalogue of Biblical allusion and quotations, are each and all substantial accessories
　　to the knowledge of the author."—DR. RICHARD GARNETT, in the *Illustrated
　　London News.*

WATSON (E. H. LACON).

　　THE UNCONSCIOUS HUMOURIST, AND OTHER ESSAYS.
　　　　　　　　　　　　　　　　　　　　　　　　[In preparation.

*[Mr. Wedmore's Short Stories.　New and Uniform Issue.
　　　Crown 8vo., each Volume 3s. 6d. net.]*

WEDMORE (FREDERICK).

　　PASTORALS OF FRANCE.　Fourth Edition.　Crown 8vo.
　　　　3*s.* 6*d. net.*　　　　　　　　　　　　　　　*[Ready.*

　　New York: Charles Scribner's Sons.

　　　"A writer in whom delicacy of literary touch is united with an almost disem-
　　bodied fineness of sentiment."—*Athenæum.*

　　　"Of singular quaintness and beauty."—*Contemporary Review.*

　　　"The stories are exquisitely told."—*The World.*

　　　"Delicious idylls, written with Mr. Wedmore's fascinating command of
　　sympathetic incident, and with his characteristic charm of style."—*Illustrated London
　　News.*

　　　"The publication of the 'Pastorals' may be said to have revealed, not only a new
　　talent, but a new literary *genre.* . . The charm of the writing never fails."—*Bookman*

　　　"In their simplicity, their tenderness, their quietude, their truthfulness to the
　　remote life that they depict, 'Pastorals of France' are almost perfect."—*Spectator.*

WEDMORE (FREDERICK)—continued.

RENUNCIATIONS. Third Edition. With a Portrait by
J. J. SHANNON. Cr. 8vo. 3s. 6d. net. [Ready.

New York: Charles Scribner's Sons.

" These are clever studies in polite realism. '—*Athenæum.*

" They are quite unusual. The picture of Richard Pelse, with his one moment of romance, is exquisite."—*St. James's Gazette.*

" ' The Chemist in the Suburbs,' in ' Renunciations,' is a pure joy. . . . The story of Richard Pelse's life is told with a power not unworthy of the now disabled hand that drew for us the lonely old age of M. Parent."—MR. TRAILL, in *The New Review.*

" The book belongs to the highest order of imaginative work. ' Renunciations ' are studies from the life—pictures which make plain to us some of the innermost workings of the heart."—*Academy.*

" Mr. Wedmore has gained for himself an enviable reputation. His style has distinction, has form. He has the poet's secret now to bring out the beauty of common things. . . . ' The Chemist in the Suburbs,' in ' Renunciations,' is his masterpiece."—*Saturday Review.*

" We congratulate Mr. Wedmore on his vivid, wholesome, and artistic work, so full of suppressed feeling and of quiet strength."—*Standard.*

ENGLISH EPISODES. Second Edition. Cr. 8vo. 3s. 6d.
net. [Ready.

New York: Charles Scribner's Sons.|

" Distinction is the characteristic of Mr. Wedmore's manner. These things remain on the mind as things seen ; not read of."—*Daily News.*

" A penetrating insight, a fine pathos. Mr. Wedmore is a peculiarly fine and sane and carefully deliberate artist."—*Westminster Gazette.*

" In ' English Episodes ' we have another proof of Mr. Wedmore's unique position among the writers of fiction of the day. We hardly think of his short volumes as ' stories,' but rather as life-secrets and hearts' blood, crystalised somehow, and, in their jewel-form, cut with exceeding skill by the hand of a master-workman.' . . The faultless episode of the ' Vicar of Pimlico ' is the best in loftiness of purpose and keeness of interest ; but the ' Fitting Obsequies ' is its equal on different lines, and deserves to be a classic."—*World.*

" ' English Episodes ' are worthy successors of ' Pastorals ' and ' Renunciations,' and with them should represent a permanent addition to Literature."—*Academy.*

There may also be had the Collected Edition (1893) of "Pastorals of France" and "Renunciations," with Title-page by John Fulleylove, R.I. 5s. net.

WICKSTEED (P. H., Warden of University Hall).

DANTE : SIX SERMONS.

*** A FOURTH EDITION. (Unaltered Reprint). Cr. 8vo. 2s. net.

" It is impossible not to be struck with the reality and earnestness with which Mr. Wicksteed seeks to do justice to what are the supreme elements of the *Commedia,* its spiritual significance, and the depth and insight of its moral teaching."—*Guardian.*

WYNNE (FRANCES).

WHISPER! A Volume of Verse. Fcap. 8vo. buckram. 2s. 6d. net.

Transferred by the Author to the present Publisher.

"A little volume of singularly sweet and graceful poems, hardly one of which can be read by any lover of poetry without definite pleasure, and everyone who reads either of them without is, we venture to say, unable to appreciate that play of light and shadow on the heart of man which is of the very essence of poetry."—*Spectator.*

"The book includes, to my humble taste, many very charming pieces, musical, simple, straightforward and not 'as sad as night.' It is long since I have read a more agreeable volume of verse, successful up to the measure of its aims and ambitions."—MR. ANDREW LANG, in *Longman's Magazine.*

YEATS (W. B.).

THE SHADOWY WATERS. A Poetic Play. [*In preparation.*

THE WIND AMONG THE REEDS (Poems). [*In preparation.*

MR. ELKIN MATHEWS *holds likewise the only copies of the following Books printed at the Private Press of the* REV. C. HENRY DANIEL, *Fellow of Worcester College, Oxford.*

BRIDGES (ROBERT).

THE GROWTH OF LOVE. Printed in Fell's old English type, on Whatman paper. 100 copies. Fcap. 4to. £2. 12s. 6d. net.   [*Very few remain.*

SHORTER POEMS. Printed in Fell's old English type, on Whatman paper. 100 copies. Five Parts. Fcap. 4to. £2. 12s. 6d. net.   [*Very few remain.*

HYMNI ECCLESIÆ CVRA HENRICI DANIEL.

Small 8vo. (1882), £1. 15s. net.

BLAKE HIS SONGS OF INNOCENCE

Sq. 16mo. 100 copies only. 12s. 6d. net.

MILTON ODE ON THE NATIVITY.

Sq. 16mo. 10s. 6d. net.

LONDON   VIGO STREET, W.

www.ingramcontent.com/pod-product-compliance
Lightning Source LLC
Chambersburg PA
CBHW030626270326
41927CB00007B/1329